SECURE YOUR HOME

SECURE YOUR HOME

ALEXA STACE

HAMLYN

First published in 1990 by
The Hamlyn Publishing Group Limited,
a division of the Octopus Publishing Group,
Michelin House, 81 Fulham Road,
London SW3 6RB

ISBN 0 600 57067 3

Typeset by SX Composing Ltd, Rayleigh, Essex
Printed and bound in Great Britain by Collins, Glasgow

Contents

Introduction

Crime, particularly crime against property, has been a growing problem over the last 30 years. In Britain, one home in 40 has been burgled, and in London that figure rises to one in 13. Yet many people still feel 'it couldn't happen to me', in spite of all the evidence to the contrary. These are the people who have no insurance cover, and whose homes are only too easy to break into.

Having your home invaded by burglers or vandals is a nasty, even traumatic experience. Even if you are fully insured (and few people are) financial compensation will never make up for the loss of family momentoes, the destruction of important papers or photographs. Being broken into is bad enough, but burglars, squatters or vandals can also wreak fearful havoc in your home.

But all is not gloom – simply by becoming more aware of the problem, you can help to reduce it. It is important to understand the nature of this crime: for the most part it is neither pre-planned nor carried out by professionals. Crimes against property are opportunist, committed mainly by adolescents and young men – the peak age for offenders is 15.

There is a lot the householder can do to help himself, particularly by cutting down the opportunities for these criminals. Amazingly, the police say that in 30 per cent of domestic burglaries the burglar or intruder simply walked in, because the owners had left a door or window unlocked.

No one has to live in a state of siege, but by becoming more security conscious you can cut down the opportunities for crime dramatically, and even reverse the trend – in your home, in your family and in the neighbourhood.

ONE

The Vulnerable Points

Most burglaries are opportunist – and the burglar will always go for the property that is easy to break into, the house that he can get into quickly and quietly, without being seen.

A very useful exercise is to put yourself into the burglar's shoes. Stand outside your house or flat next time you come back from work or from a shopping trip and imagine that you have lost your keys; how easy would it be to break in? Is the side window or kitchen window open? Is there a side gate round to the back, where you can get in through the patio door, or is the garage always left unlocked, with an internal door giving access to the house? Is the lock on your front door the simple cylinder type, so that all that is required is a credit card to slip the lock? Or can you get in by breaking a small pane of glass in an adjacent window and reaching in to undo the latch? Or is it easier just to break the window, reach in to undo the window catch and climb in? You may well be horrified at how easy it is.

Even if you have locked up properly, so that you would need to break a window to get in, you are still not burglar-proof. If all the burglar has to do is to break the glass (or use a glass cutter to quietly take out a pane of glass) and then reach through to open the door or window, you are still very vulnerable. Examine each area in detail.

The garden

Your garden may offer peace and seclusion, but it can also provide a perfect haven for the burglar, where he can work unseen and undisturbed. Hedges planted to screen the windows from passers-by will also provide a screen for the burglar trying to break in. Take a walk round and look for low or sagging fences where anyone could easily climb over. An additional deterrent is to plant a thorny hedge or climber along the fence. Is the back gate strong enough, and is it kept locked? The garden shed or outhouse should also be kept locked. They are usually full of tools and ladders that the burglar would find very useful for helping him to break in.

Are there trees growing close to the house, or ivy growing up the walls? An agile burglar (and most of them are) can use a tree or thickly growing ivy as a ladder to reach a window, or the roof of a garage or extension. Any windows that can be reached that way will have to be kept locked – including balcony, fanlight, skylight and lavatory windows. Never make the mistake of thinking that a small window is safe because no one could squeeze through. Your burglar may be a slim 12-year-old, or a small child who has been lifted up to wriggle through a window and then open a door or window to the others.

Side and back doors

Burglars like these because they can enter with less risk of being seen. If there is a side passage to the house, make sure access is difficult. It should have a strong, high gate across the passage and the gate should be kept locked and bolted top and bottom. It also creates a psychological barrier – and no burglar wants to risk attention by climbing a 6ft (1.8 metre) gate. If you share an alleyway with a neighbour, suggest sharing the cost of installing a strong gate and fitting it with locks and bolts.

Patios

Patio doors and French windows are particularly vulnerable – burglars love them! It's usually only too easy for them to break a small piece of glass and reach in to undo the catch, or even to lift the sliding patio doors out of their runners. Ideally, patio windows should be fitted with toughened glass and special locks, top and bottom, so that if the burglar breaks the glass and reaches in, he still can't unlock the door or lift the doors out of their runners. French windows should have rack bolts, or key-operated metal bolts, top and bottom, together with a mortise deadlock where the doors meet.

Windows

All ground-floor windows are at risk as well as any windows that can easily be reached via a flat roof or drainpipe, and they should all be fitted with locks. The most vulnerable are louvred windows and leaded lights. The glass slats of louvres are easily lifted from their frames. Glue the slats in position with an epoxy resin, and fit a special louvre lock, or better still, replace them with fixed glass. Where there are small leaded lights, making it easy for the burglar to break the pane and reach in, it is important to have window locks, rather than catches that can be unfastened.

The garage

Never leave the garage unlocked, especially if there is a connecting door to the house. A thief can let himself in and then work on the inner door in privacy. Never drive off and leave the garage standing open and empty, advertising your absence. Remember too that garages often provide access to tools and ladders, to help the burglar break in or climb in. Lock ladders away, or padlock them horizontally to a stout bracket on an outside wall.

Drainpipes

Think of drainpipes as ladders and look carefully at all windows, including fanlights and skylights, that could be reached that way. Fit locking catches to all these windows and remember to lock them whenever you go out. To make things more difficult, you can treat metal (but not plastic) drainpipes with a special anti-climb paint which makes the pipe greasy and leaves a sticky deposit on the hands.

The front door

A surprising number of burglars get in through the front door. And if the burglar can open this quickly and easily, he can then carry out bulky items – such as a video – with no problems. The favourite ploy of a burglar is simply to knock at the door to see if anyone is in. In a suburban street in mid-afternoon there may be very few people around. A burglar who looks like a legitimate caller – council workman, say, or a canvasser with a clipboard, will attract little attention. If there is someone in, he can always pretend to have been given the wrong address.

Your aim must therefore be to make the front door as fortress-like as possible. To the would-be burglar the simple cylinder rim latch on the average front door is a very inviting target. He can easily open it either with a strip of plastic or mica such as a credit card, or by forcing the door with a jemmy, or by breaking an adjacent window and reaching in to undo the catch.

You should fit the front door with a 5-lever mortise dead-lock, if possible, and at least have a rim latch with a security deadlock (see page 19), so that even if he gets in by the window he cannot open the door from the inside. If the door is wholly or partly of glass it is obviously more vulnerable. The answer – apart from totally replacing the door – is to fit tough-ened glass or to fit a wrought iron grille behind the glass. This is a good deterrent, making it obvious you mean business, and can be quite ornamental.

Flats present a particular problem. The front door of a flat is often rather thin and not as strong as the door of a house. If an intruder manages to get through the front door of a block of flats, perhaps by bluffing his way in, he may find it child's play to slip the lock of the flat, or even to break down the door. Apart from replacing the door completely, the answer is to strengthen the door frame with steel strips and hinge bolts (see page 24). Fit a security deadlock, or a 5-lever mor-tise lock, so that the door cannot be slipped or forced open.

Porches

A porch can be a second line of defence – no burglar wants to break through two doors to get into a house. So long as your porch is fitted with a mortise lock, and is kept locked, you will have double protection. Remember though that a porch that virtually conceals the front door will enable a thief to work on the door without fear of being seen. Make sure there is a good light in the porch and cut back any bushes or creepers that shield the porch from view from the road. Anyone standing in a glass porch is more visible, but remember that letters, circulars etc. lying on the floor inside can advertise your absence to the opportunist burglar. The answer is to fit a box (not wire) behind the front door.

Cellars and basements

Older properties often have cellars or basements with windows or doors leading into the garden or a downstairs area in front of the house. This part of the house is often converted into a separate flat, otherwise it is probably used as a storage area. The doors leading from the cellar up into the house should of course be kept locked and bolted at all times, but it is equally important to secure any doors or windows giving access to the cellar or basement from outside. The cellar is likely to be full of tools and ladders that the burglar will find extremely useful in helping him break into the rest of the house. And the tools themselves, including gardening equipment such as hedge trimmers, electric saws, mowers etc. would be expensive to replace if stolen.

Because it is rarely used, except in the summer, and is below ground level, the basement or cellar door is likely to be in poor condition. Check the door and window frames for rot and replace them if necessary – there is little point in locking them if the wood is rotten so that a good kick or push will loosen them. The door should be secured with bolts as well as a good mortise lock, and the windows should also have locking catches fitted.

Lighting

Remember that burglars don't like the limelight. Make sure that the outside of your house, including the porch, front and back doors, side entrance, patio and French windows etc., are well lit after dark.

Exterior lights controlled by a passive infra-red sensor give very good protection against prowlers – this sensor detects the heat given off by a body entering its field of view and immediately switches on the lights. A variable time switch turns them off again after a pre-set length of time. When you are on holiday, make sure that selected interior lights come on in the evening with a time switch (see page 76) – a dark, obviously empty house is a very tempting target for the opportunist burglar.

Security checklist

A lot of anti-burglar strategy is commonsense. Here is a list of helpful do's and don'ts.

- Always lock up, even if you are just popping round to the local shops.

- If you lose your keys, and they are later returned, always change the locks. Never carry an address tag with your keys, and don't keep them in a bag that could lead the finder to your home.

- Always change the locks when you move house. It is a good opportunity to fit a secure deadlock front and back and besides, you don't know who might have spare keys.

- Never leave keys on a string behind the letterbox, or under the doormat, flowerpot, on a window ledge etc. Burglars know all the hiding places. The best plan is to leave the key with a neighbour you trust.

- Never let strangers into your house without checking their credentials, even if they claim to be police. If in doubt, ask them to call back later while you ring to check.

■ Avoid the tell-tale signs of absence – milk bottles on the doorstep, newspapers stuck in the letterbox, grass uncut. Cancel the milk and papers when you go away, and ask a neighbour to keep an eye on things. If you are going away for some time, arrange for a friend to cut the grass and keep the garden tidy.

■ Draw the curtains after dark and keep the porch well lit. If you are going out, leave a light on in the kitchen or bedroom, and draw the blinds.

■ Don't leave valuable equipment – camerers, stereos, videos, computer equipment etc. – in full view of the front windows – someone may not be able to resist temptation.

■ Only put initials in the telephone directory or on the nameplate so that no one knows if a man or woman lives there.

■ Beware of sneak thieves in warm weather, when you are likely to have doors and windows open a lot. If you are going to be in in the garden all afternoon, make sure the front door and windows are locked – you may not hear an intruder.

■ If window cleaners or other workmen call looking for jobs, check out their credentials before letting them into the house. Ask for their card or telephone number, and ask for references.

■ Don't drive off and leave an empty garage open, advertising the fact that you are not in the house. It gives a would-be thief access to items such as ladders and tools.

TWO

Doors

Your front and back doors must be strong enough to keep out burglars, but at the same time they should keep your property in. It's not enough to have a securely locked and bolted front door if the locks are rudimentary – such as a non-deadlocking cylinder rim latch on the front door and a 2-lever mortise lock on the back door. If a burglar then gets in by breaking a window and climbing in, he will have no trouble leaving with your TV, stereo etc. through whichever door he chooses. In other words, your doors should not be unlockable from the inside (the key being removed) so that the burglar has to go out the way he came in, preferably empty-handed.

But before thinking about locks, look at the door itself. If the door is weak and flimsy, locks and bolts are a waste of time. Pay particular attention to the front door if you live in a flat. This is the most vulnerable point in a flat, and often the flat door is not as strong and thick as the main outside door. If your door seems thin and flimsy, replace it and fit hinge bolts (page 24) and steel strips (page 15). As a rule, an external door should have a minimum thickness of 1¾in (44mm). Check outside doors for rot, and make sure the door frame is firmly fixed in the opening.

Ideally, your front door should be panelled, not flush, with the panels made of solid wood. Glass panels are much less secure (the burglar can break the glass and reach in to open the door – unless you have fitted a mortise lock). If you need glass to give light, make sure it is toughened safety glass. Leaded lights are a particularly weak spot in a front door, and should be reinforced with metal bars behind.

One way of adding considerably to the strength of a door is to attach steel reinforcing strips. These are specially made steel strips which are screwed down both sides of a door frame. They are quite unobtrusive, and are one of the security devices often specified by insurance companies.

For high-risk areas, you can fit a steel sheet which is bolted to the outside of the door. This makes your door impregnable, but make sure the keys can easily be found in the case of fire, as in the past the Fire Brigade have had difficulty breaking down these doors without special equipment.

Locks

Once you have made sure the door is strong enough, look at the locks. For a front door, a nightlatch or cylinder rim latch is usually fitted as a convenient way of opening and closing the door quickly. But for security, you must be able to deadlock the latch, so that the bolt cannot be moved back unless the key is used. The back door should be fitted with a good quality mortise lock, and bolts top and bottom. These are the absolute minimum requirements. As you will see below, there are many other, more stringent security precautions you can take.

Rim locks

The rim latch is the most common kind of lock for a front door. Rim locks screw to the surface of the door and are easy to fit. They have a spring-operated latch which automatically springs back when the door is shut. The latch is operated by a key from the outside, and a knob from the inside. In its basic form this lock offers little security, because it is so easily opened – the burglar can smash a pane of glass and reach in to turn the knob, or push back the springbolt with a piece of flexible plastic, such as the ubiquitous credit card.

For perfect security, you need an automatic deadlock which can be locked from outside or inside, and a springbolt with a mechanism that prevents the bolt being forced back – this will foil the thief who either breaks the glass and turns the handle from the inside, or tries to force the door with a jemmy. If your front door has glass panels, latches that dead-lock are essential. Don't leave the keys to the deadlock lying around for the burglar to find. Keep them in a safe place where you can find them quickly in case of fire.

The lock body is fitted to the face of the door, and it is important that the hole for the cylinder is correctly positioned to ensure smooth operation of the latch. For this purpose, a paper template is often provided for marking the hole position (1a) – a bradawl is a suitable tool to use. After drilling a hole of the specified diameter, position the cylinder from outside the door and mark where the connecting bar needs to be cut (1b); notches are usually cut in the bar which can simply be snapped off at the required point with a pair of pliers. The lock body is secured to a backplate which must be screwed squarely to the door (1c), and the cylinder is then secured to the backplate (1d); it helps to insert the key in the cylinder to hold it steady. The lock body engages on a locating peg on the backplate and is secured at the edge with small screws (1e). The catch plate, or staple, must align exactly with the lock. After marking the position on the door frame (1f), hold the

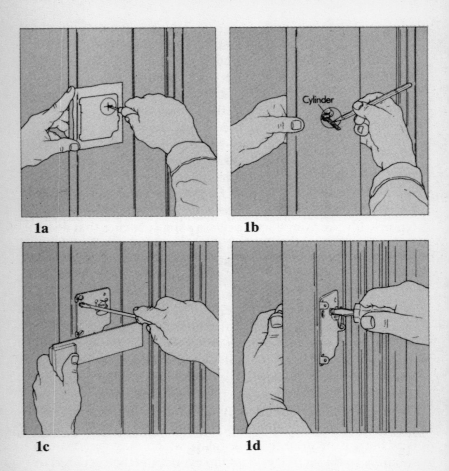

1a

1b

1c

1d

staple against the lines and mark round the edge (**1g**) before chiselling out a recess for the plate. Check the operation of the lock *before* screwing the staple to the frame (**1h**) so that any adjustments can be made without the need to fill screw-holes.

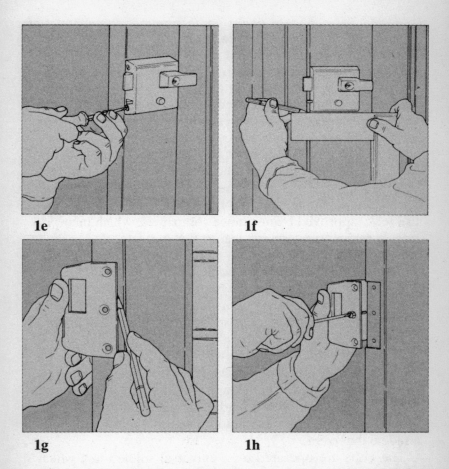

1e

1f

1g

1h

If you move house, or if your keys are stolen, it is a good idea to change the locks. Some lock firms, such as Ingersoll and Banhams, have a system of locks with registered keys, so that if you lose your keys it is impossible for the person who finds them to have extra ones cut before handing them back.

Mortise locks

For added security, external doors need a mortise lock, ideally one which meets British Standard 3621. The body of a mortise lock is embedded in the thickness of the door, invisible when the door is closed, making it less likely to be forced or tampered with. Most mortise locks are operated by levers, and the number of levers determines the level of security. The more levers there are, the greater the number of key variations and the more secure the lock, making it difficult to pick. A 2-lever lock is not very secure, while a 5-lever one is. For maximum security, Banhams make a 7-lever mortise lock, approved by insurance companies, which incorporates a device to safeguard against picking.

Mortise rack bolts

These are fitted at the top and bottom of doors. They can be used as extra security and rigidity for an external door already fitted with a rim latch or mortise lock, making it virtually impossible to force. They are also ideal for internal doors, making it possible to isolate every room in the house. The rack bolt is invisible to the burglar as the key hole is on the inside. If he forces a way in through a window, he is then faced with a bolted door, with no indication of the position of the bolts. Time is an important factor to a housebreaker, so this is an ideal deterrent.

The bolts are operated by a universal splined key which winds out the bolt. Unfortunately, these bolts are now quite common, and your well-organised burglar may well carry one of these keys with him as part of his kit. However, it is possible to buy a lockable bolt, enabling the shot bolt to be locked in position – remember to remove the key.

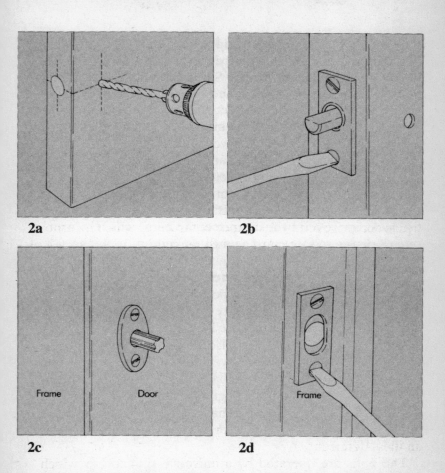

2a

2b

2c

Frame

Door

2d

Frame

Fitting a mortise rack bolt is a simple matter of drilling a hole in the edge of the door for the lock body and a hole in the inside face of the door for the key (**2a**), and securing the lock with two screws (**2b**). Extend the bolt before inserting the lock so that you have something to grip if the lock needs to be removed again. The faceplate and cover plate (see below) can be recessed to lie flush with the surface for neatness or if the door is a tight fit in the frame (which it should be for security). Screw the escutcheon over the keyhole with the key in position (**2c**) to ensure that it will turn freely. Finally, drill a hole in the door frame to accept the bolt when extended and fit the cover plate (**2d**).

Hinge bolts

Doors that open outwards are vulnerable because the hinge pins are exposed: it is easy for an intruder to knock out the pins and prise open the door from the hinge side. Even an inward-opening door can be easily forced on the hinge side if the hinges are not strong enough. The answer is to fit hinge bolts. These are strong studs, set into the hinge edge of the door, which fit into sockets in the door frame. They are quite easy to fit and will give added security against the use of force.

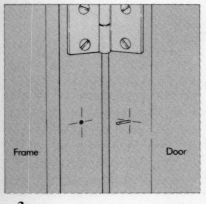

Frame   Door

3a

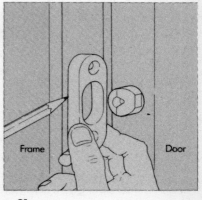

Frame   Door

3b

A pin, hammered into the edge of the door, is used to mark the corresponding position on the door frame (**3a**). Remove the pin and drill a hole for the stud in the door, then hammer it into position, protecting it with an offcut of wood. Recess the lock plate into the frame centrally over the pin mark (**3b**). Two or three bolts are sufficient to secure a door.

Door chains

These are ideal for the elderly, or the nervous. The stranger on the doorstep who then barges in is a common story. The thief may try to talk his or her way in, pretending to be from the police, electricity board, council etc. If that doesn't work the stranger may then simply force his way in, especially if the householder is weak or elderly. With a door chain access is restricted while you speak to the person outside. If you don't like the look of him or her, or their story sounds fishy, simply shut the door – they cannot get past the chain. It restricts

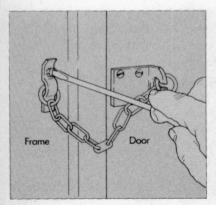

Frame   Door

4a

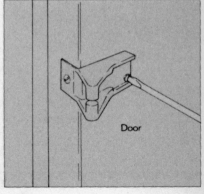

Door

4b

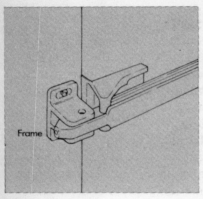

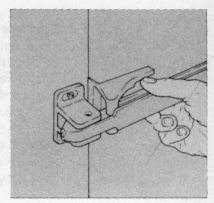

4c   **4d**

the amount a door can be opened to about 2ins (5cm).

The police recommend asking for the credentials of anyone who claims to be from an official body such as the police or the gas board, etc. With a chain, you can simply leave them standing on the doorstep while you go off to phone the office and check their story. But remember the old adage that a chain is as strong as its weakest link – and make sure that the chain that you buy is a really heavy one. The staple (to which the chain is attached) is screwed to the door frame and the ring plate is attached to the door (**4a**), so that when the chain is not in use it hangs from the door frame. Once it is in position, train yourself to use it at all times.

A more solid version of the door chain is the door limiter which consists of a pivoted bar that is secured (when in use) in a guide attached to the edge of the door (**4b**). The staple on which the bar pivots is screwed to the door frame (**4c**) in such a position as to allow the bar to be removed from the guide only when the door is fully closed (**4d**).

Surface bolts

It is officially recommended that surface bolts should be fitted at the top and bottom of all external doors, for use at night. They are particularly useful for garages, back doors, side gates, garden gates etc. where the intruder might try to force his way in unseen. There are two types (**5a**): tower bolts (centre); and barrel bolts. Various finishes are available in both types. Make sure the bolts are attached with strong screws – small weak ones are easily wrenched out. The bolts will give greater security if they are mounted so as to shoot into the head and sill of the frame (**5b**), dispensing with the staples. A recessed cover plate over the hole makes this arrangement even stronger.

Steel grilles and gates

A good way to strengthen a glass door, or a door with glass panels, is to fit a steel or wrought-iron security grille. These

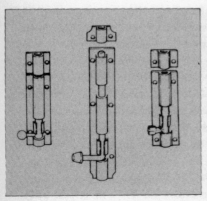

5a

5b

come in a variety of patterns and can be made to measure. Provided the door is securely locked, the thief is then helpless: even if he breaks the glass and can reach in, he will get no further. Another high-security device for a vulnerable door is a collapsible steel gate, with its own tracking, which can be pushed back out of sight when not in use. These usually come with their own high security lock.

Door viewers

Door viewers are ideal for the elderly or nervous, because you can usually examine callers without their being aware of the fact and without having to open the door. Personal confrontation is thus avoided and you have the added advantage that they cannot tell anything about the person inside – whether the occupant is a frail old lady, for example – and sometimes even whether there is anyone inside at all.

A door viewer is a spyhole consisting of a small wide-angle lens and usually fitted in the middle of the door. It should be fitted at a level which is workable for all the occupants of the home who are likely to need to use it. Don't fit it too high, or children and the elderly might not be able to use it.

The image is a little distorted by the wide-angle effect – most viewers have a field of view of 160° to 190° – but it needs to be wide so that it is impossible for anyone (an accomplice trying to hide, for example) to press himself/herself against the wall beside the door without being seen. Make sure you have a good light outside the door, so that callers can be seen at night, otherwise it will be difficult to tell friend from foe.

The door viewer should be used in conjunction with a door chain, and certainly not as a substitute for it. Unless you have positively identified your caller as someone you know and

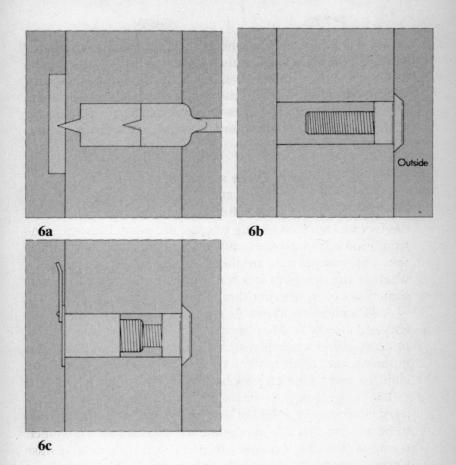

6a

6b

Outside

6c

trust, it would be advisable to check that the door chain or
door limiter is also in use before you open the door: a re-
cognisable uniform, for example, is no guarantee of identity.

The door viewer is easy to install and simply involves drilling a hole in the door (**6a**); a piece of scrap wood held against

the face of the door will prevent the wood from splintering when the drill bit breaks through. Most viewers are in two parts which screw together, so they can be fitted to doors with a wide range of thickness. Position the outside section **(6b)** and screw the inside section to it until hand-tight **(6c)**; if a cover is fitted to the inside section, rotate it so that the pivot is at the top.

THREE

Windows

The bad news is that the windows are the most vulnerable places in the home – most burglars, as many as two out of three, make their entry that way, all too frequently through a window left unfastened or unlocked. The good news is that there is a lot you can do to make them secure.

Burglars don't like locked windows, because breaking glass attracts attention. Also, even if they smash the window, they won't be able to open it, which means climbing in past broken glass. And if you have locked the front and back door, and removed the key, they won't be able to carry your possessions out of the door, but will have to get out the way they came in – past broken glass. All of which is a great deterrent – the burglar who finds the windows locked may well decide to try elsewhere.

Attend to the most vulnerable windows first – ground floor windows, windows which can't be seen from the street, and windows which can be reached from a drainpipe or flat roof, including toilet windows, fanlights and skylights. These small windows (which you might think are too small for a burglar to get through) are often the biggest security risk. Never leave them open, even when you are only leaving the house for a short time. Remember that a lot of burglaries are opportunist, spur-of-the-moment affairs, taking advantage of some one's carelessness, and that your burglar might be a slim, agile teenager who can easily wriggle through even the smallest window.

Wooden casement windows

Casement windows can be hinged at the sides, at the top or in the middle. These windows should have key-operated locks, firmly screwed in so that they won't be opened if the catch is forced. There are a variety of casement locks on the market. Some lock automatically. For a top-hung casement window you can fit a window stay lock which will hold the window closed, or slightly open, and these are often fitted as a safety precaution for young children, to prevent them climbing, or falling, out.

These locks are best used in conjunction with a mortise rack bolt, for maximum security. Just like the door bolt, the window rack bolt is fitted into the edge of the window frame.

7a

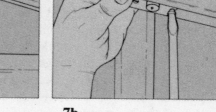

7b

A serrated key is used to wind the bolt out into the frame. The key is removed after use and the bolt cannot be pushed back without it.

The number of bolts you need depends on the kind of window. For a small, side-hung window you only need one bolt, fitted close to the centre of the frame. For a large side-hung window you will need two bolts, top and bottom. For a top-hung window you will need two bolts at the bottom, one on each side.

These locks are simply a smaller version of the type for doors (see page 00) and are fitted in the same way: drill the hinged casement to take the lock body (7a), and drill a hole for the key; screw the lock to the casement after cutting a recess for the faceplate (7b); fit the escutcheon, drill the frame to accept the extended bolt, and recess and fit the cover plate (7c).

NOTE: Many windows only open outwards, and access

7c

may be a problem. Rather than trying to work from a ladder, it is much easier, and safer, to remove the casement from its hinges, and fit the lock and escutcheon on a workbench; then rehang the window, operate the bolt to mark the frame, and complete the fitting. If you must work from a ladder, make absolutely sure that it is firmly secured top and bottom and standing on firm ground.

Sash windows

Sash windows have always been regarded as child's play to open – and some of them still are. Often all the burglar has to do is insert a thin metal bar or blade between the sashes and knock back the arm of the fastener. Modern fasteners, such as the Brighton screw-down type, and the fitch fastener, cannot be knocked back, so the job is no longer so easy, but if the window is broken, it is still possible for the fastener to be undone by hand. The only answer is to fit window locks.

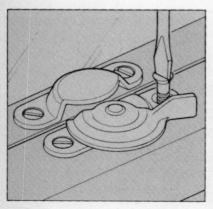

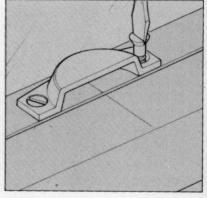

8a　　　　　　　　　　**8b**

One of the simplest and most effective locks for a sash window is the screw lock. This key-operated lock simply screws the meeting rails of the upper and lower sashes together, effectively preventing them from being forced apart. Another version of this screw enables the window to be opened up to 4in (10cm) for ventilation while still locked.

Another easily fitted lock is the locking catch, which replaces the conventional fitch fastener on the top and bottom meeting rails. The catch operates in just the same way as the fitch, but is then locked in position when the key is removed. To fit it, remove the existing catch and catch plate (**8a**) and screw the new catch plate to the centre of the outer (upper) sash meeting rail (**8b**). Position and fasten the locking catch to locate it and screw it to the inner (lower) sash meeting rail (**8c**).

The more elaborate sash window lock is fitted to the top rail of the lower sash, at the side, and a slotted plate is fitted to the

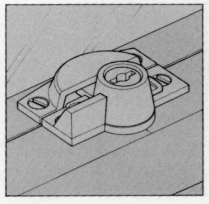

8c

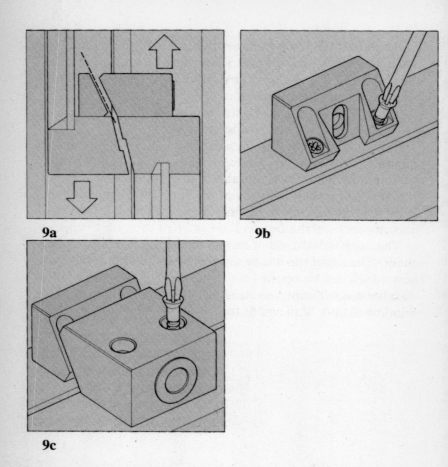

9a

9b

9c

top sash. Turning the key shoots the bolt into the slotted plate and the window is then immovable. The slotted plate has two positions so the window can be locked open for ventilation.

The sash window lock illustrated has a clenching action when the two parts are secured by the key **(9a)**. Mount the catch plate on the outer sash near the catch (**9b**), or mount one each side on larger windows. Screw the lock body to the inner sash (**9c**) and fit cover plugs over the screws so that it cannot be removed.

Metal windows

What kind of lock you fit on a metal window will depend on whether it is a steel or aluminium frame. It is often difficult to fit standard metal locks in aluminium windows – it is best either to buy locks specially made for aluminium windows, or, if it is a replacement window, to make sure it is fitted with security locks in the factory.

The most usual kind of metal window is the hinged casement. The small top window is top hung and has a fastening stay which can be opened for ventilation. The main window also has a ventilation stay, and a cockspur handle to hold the window closed. You can fit locks to hold the ventilation stay

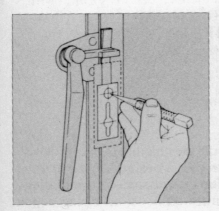

10a

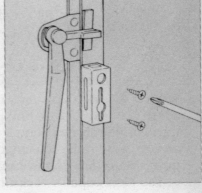

10b

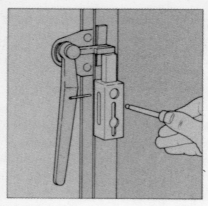

10c

closed, and locks to prevent the cockspur handle being opened.

A cockspur handle bolt is screwed to the window frame. The hole positions are marked through a paper template using a centre punch (**10a**), and the lock body is secured with two self-tapping screws (**10b**). The bolt may be secured in the lock with a small pin (**10c**), and it is important to fit any cover plugs supplied over the screws so that they cannot be removed.

Stay locks are simple clamp-on devices which hold the ventilation stay in the closed position. The best kind are key-operated so that they cannot be easily removed by an intruder. The method of fitting and the stay lock used will depend on the type of stay. If the stay has holes that fit over securing pegs, fit the type that replaces one of the pegs (**11a**); to secure the window, fasten the stay and screw the stay stop into the lock using the special key (**11b**). If the stay has no holes, or the pegs cannot be unscrewed, fit the type that

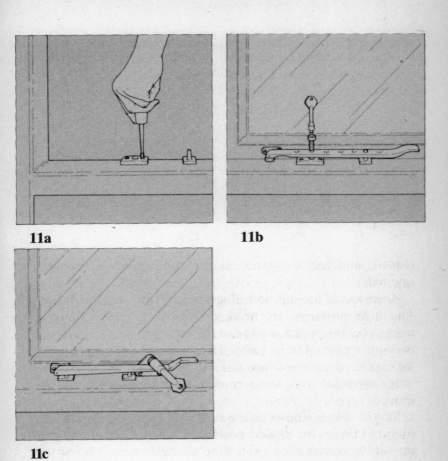

11a

11b

11c

clamps the stay down on the existing stay supports (**11c**); screw the lock to the fixed frame so that, when the stop is in position, the stay cannot be lifted at all.

For the cockspur handle fit a key-operated bolt, just below the handle, which will prevent it being opened if the window

12a   **12b**

is broken. There are also various metal window locks which are fitted with screws to the window frame. Some high security ones have a flush fitting rebate to prevent them being prised off the frame, and no accessible fixing screws. The kind with a pivoting lock has a hinged catch which is fitted on to the opening frame. It locks on to a staple fitted to the fixed frame by means of a screw-down key.

It is possible to fit locks on metal frames yourself, but the more solid old-fashioned windows were made of fairly tough steel and drilling holes in them is not always as simple as it might at first appear. You need a bit that is hard enough for the metal, and an old hand-drill or slow electric drill – and you need accuracy and patience. To stop the drill bit from skidding, use a punch to make a dent in the metal.

Sliding windows

For sliding windows or patio doors, fit a key-operated window lock which screws on to the edge of the inside window. When

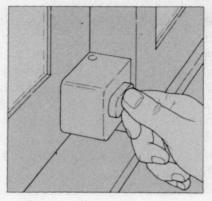

12c

in operation a bolt locks it on to the outer window. For a large patio window fit locks top and bottom (**12a**), either at the outer edge of the sliding door or where the two doors meet. The lock should prevent the door from being lifted out of its track. The mounting plate is attached to the edge of the door with self-tapping screws (**12b**) and operation is by a push bolt (**12c**) which is released by the key. Remember that patio doors are regarded as the burglar's dream – so be warned.

French windows

If the French windows are timber-framed first check that they have not been weakened with wood rot. If they are badly decayed, it would be advisable to fit new doors. It is also advisable to install toughened or laminated glass – far too many burglaries still occur through old-fashioned French windows fitted with ordinary glass and inadequate locks, simply carried out at a time when no one is about to hear the noise.

Once you have checked the strength of the windows,

install rack bolts top and bottom, and a mortise lock where the doors meet.

One weak spot about outward-opening doors is that the hinge pins can be knocked out and the doors prised open on the hinge side. To strengthen the hinges, fit hinge bolts in the hinge edge of the door (see page 24) close to the hinges.

For metal-framed French windows, fit key-operated bolts for metal windows top and bottom. The door with the latch should also have two bolts close to the top and bottom.

Louvre windows

Louvre windows are very insecure and it is often very easy for an intruder to lift the strips of glass out of their frames. Ideally, they should never be fitted to ground floor windows or to any windows that are easily reached. If you live in a high-risk area think seriously about having them replaced with a conventional window fitted with a good window lock. To make them more secure in the meantime, cover them with metal security grilles or change the blades to laminated safety glass and glue them in position using strong epoxy resin adhesive.

Double glazing

Double glazing does not in itself make a window more secure, but it undoubtedly acts as a deterrent. The burglar now has two lots of glass to break, taking a lot longer and making a lot more noise. A lot depends on the type of double glazing fitted. In the case of made-to-measure replacement windows and sealed units, it all depends on the quality of the locks fitted by the manufacturer – it is worth looking carefully at this point before deciding on a double glazing system.

The most common kind of double glazing fitted is second-ary glazing, where a separate pane of glass or plastic is fitted to the inside of the existing window frame. From the security point of view, glass is preferable to plastic, since breaking glass makes more noise and is much more dangerous. Again, it all comes down to the kind of locks fitted to keep the glazing closed.

Shutters

Older properties (turn-of-the-century or earlier) sometimes still have their original wooden shutters, fitted inside and de-signed to fold back when not in use into recesses either side of the window. If your house was fitted with these shutters, have them repaired if need be and make sure you use them. They are almost as good as double glazing in conserving heat and will undoubtedly act as a very effective barrier, providing they still have the internal bar holding them in position. The only problem is that if you are away for days at a time – on holiday, for example – leaving the shutters up advertises the fact that the house is empty. You must then make doubly sure that other windows and doors are securely locked and ask a neighbour to keep an eye on the property for you.

Roller shutters

The modern equivalent of wooden shutters are foam-filled roller shutters, which can be fitted internally or externally. They are operated from inside the house either by a simple cord pull or an electric motor. These modern shutters are very attractive in appearance and come in a wide range of colours.

Roller shutters are widely used on the Continent where it is recognised that they are better insulators than double glazing.

Indeed in Belgium and West Germany they are fitted by law on all new houses, to reduce heat loss and conserve fuel. And in the summer the foam-filled shutters keep the house cool, by preventing the sun's rays penetrating further than the glass.

But the real advantage of these shutters is the extra security they provide, especially for vulnerable windows, including patios and glass doors. Full-length shutters like these are a real deterrent to would-be intruders, and they don't mean that you have to have your windows locked at all times. As on the Continent, you can have the shutters down and the windows open in the summer, keeping the house cool during the day but denying access to burglars. They can also be used on warm evenings with the windows open and closed as darkness approaches. They are not at all complicated to operate – they are as easy to open and close as curtains, and can be fitted with locking mechanisms.

Metal grilles

For extra security fit metal grilles over particularly vulnerable windows. There is a wide range of these grilles, both ready-to-assemble for the DIY expert, and ones that are made-to-measure. They can be diamond mesh, barred, strapping (for Georgian type windows) and ornamental cast iron. Some are available hinged, to make window cleaning easier. Another option for French windows etc. is a collapsible steel gate with its own high security lock. These gates come with their own tracking and can be pushed back out of sight when not in use.

FOUR

Garages, Sheds and Outhouses

When you are considering home security, it's easy to forget that it extends beyond the front and back doors. It should, in fact extend to the outermost perimeter of your property, covering the garden, the garage and any sheds or outhouses.

If you have a garden, it should not be too easy to get into. If it's hard to get into the garden, it's that much harder to get into the house, and that could be a deterrent in itself.

Moroever, garages, garden sheds, outhouses etc. often contain valuable equipment. Your garage, for example, apart from cars and motorbikes, may well contain bicycles, tool sets, DIY equipment, ladders, lawnmowers, barbecue equipment etc. Your garden shed too, probably holds tools and gardening equipment. If you are a keen gardener you may have a whole range of expensive equipment, including electric hedge-cutter, chain saw, strimmer, rotivator, hoses, wheelbarrow, etc. etc., not to mention garden furniture.

Add up the cost of replacing that lot – it could run into hundreds, probably thousands, of pounds. Even a good garden spade costs not much short of £100 these days. You may have a list of household items for insurance purposes, but do you have a list of garden tools and equipment? Can you remember exactly what you have stored in your garage or garden shed?

Outhouses, apart from storing garden equipment, or garden furniture, are often used to house a large chest freezer, because they take up so much room. A burglar might well fancy plundering that, too. Do you keep your freezer locked, or do you leave it and the outhouse unlocked, so that it's handy when you need to dash out to find something?

Walls and fences

Look at your perimeter first of all. A high wall, fence or hedge can have a big effect on the security of a house, especially if the property backs on to a park, fields or waste ground. It's not just a question of getting in – burglars like to plan their escape, and a high wall or fence might well prevent a quick exit. Don't build a wall with a flat top – it's too easy to climb. Put a row of coping bricks, which form a point, along the top: it's much harder to climb. You can also fit broken glass or barbed wire along the top, but check with your local authority first in case there are any objections.

It's better to have a low wall or fence at the front of the house, so the burglar can't work unseen. It's always a good idea to keep the front door and windows visible from the street, so that your neighbours can spot anything happening.

Check to see if any of the fences are broken or sagging. If it would be easy for someone to lever out a slat, have them repaired or strengthened. If you are putting up new fencing, choose vertical boarding, with horizontal wiring to prevent boards being levered out. Horizontal boards are too easy to climb. A picket fence with pointed palings at the top, or a tall welded wire mesh fence supported by concrete posts are also ideal, being very hard to climb.

Gates

All garden gates, front and back, should be securely locked or padlocked at night and when you are out. And don't forget the side gate – you want to prevent the burglar making a quick getaway round the side of the house. If you are installing an alarm system, it's worth considering extending it to the gate, to give an early warning of someone trying to force their way in. Make sure too that the back gate in particular is tall enough and strong enough, to prevent someone climbing over, or forcing it open.

The garage

As mentioned earlier, you should never drive off leaving your garage standing open and empty, advertising your absence. It's important to keep the garage locked, to prevent a burglar making good use of any tools and ladders stored inside, and it is doubly important if there is a connecting door from the garage through to the house. Once inside the garage, he can work unseen on the inner door, using the tools you have so thoughtfully provided.

Before considering locks and bolts, make sure that the garage door is strong enough to take them. A good mortise lock would be ideal, but if the door is too flimsy, fit a good sturdy padlock instead, with a locking bar or hasp made of hardened steel. Make sure that the hasp has a flap which comes over to cover the heads of the fixing bolts and screws, as well as the fixings of the staple. It's important to pay attention to the screws which fit a padlock – there's no point in having a padlock if the screws themselves can be undone or wrenched out easily. The same is true of strap hinges and other security fixings.

If your garage has wooden double doors, they may have a cylinder rim lock, which could easily be forced. Change to a 5-lever mortise lock, or fit a good padlock. If the door is the up-and-over kind, in most cases, it should still be possible to fit a padlock.

Pay particular attention to any connecting door from the garage or outhouse leading to the house. This could be a weak spot in your defences, and the door should be very securely locked and barred from the inside at all times. Use a 5-lever mortise lock.

Garden sheds

Sheds can be a problem because they are so often flimsy, or badly made. A thin wooden door can easily be pulled off its hinges, or a few boards can be prised open in the side. Before fitting locks or padlocks, you should consider strengthening the door, perhaps with hinge bolts (see page 24). A good fastening for a shed door is a padbolt, which is like a barrel bolt, but can be locked in the closed position with a padlock. Make sure it is firmly screwed on, and that the screws cannot be undone easily.

If the shed really seems very flimsy and you have expensive garden equipment, and nowhere else to keep it, such as the garage, or an outhouse or cellar, it might be better to invest in a new, stoutly built, shed altogether.

Windows

Make sure that valuable equipment is not visible through the windows of the shed or garage by fitting obscure glass or even painting over the glass. If you use the window for ventilation, make sure it has a key-operated lock, otherwise, if the window is never opened, it is easier and safer to simply screw the frames together.

Ladders

For obvious reasons, you must make absolutely certain that your ladders are safely locked away. Fix a steel bracket to the wall and padlock your ladders to it in the horizontal position.

FIVE

Car and Contents

Nowadays we tend to think of our car not just as a means of transport or a special piece of domestic equipment, but as a mobile extension of our personal living space. In it we often have a radio and music centre, some of our collection of compact discs or tapes, sometimes a CB radio or car telephone. In the back we carry, sometimes more or less permanently, sports gear and leisure equipment, tools and materials of trade, spare clothes or holiday suitcases. And inside we often leave, as casually as though it were on the kitchen table at home, our handbag, shopping, parcels, letters, briefcase, portable tape recorder, lap-top computer, camera, coat, gloves, and so on . . .

Yet having your car burgled is much the same as having your home burgled, and having the car itself stolen is just as unpleasant and sometimes even more inconvenient.

Car thefts – and thefts from cars – account for about a quarter of all recorded crime. Together they cost an estimated £260 million a year, not including the bill for nearly a million hours of police time.

About one in four of the 370,000 cars reported stolen in Britain each year is never recovered. Those that are recovered have often been damaged: a stolen car is 200 times more likely to be involved in an accident.

There is quite a lot you can do to make your car a much less inviting target, remembering that most car thefts are opportunist.

Locks

It may sound obvious, but do remember to lock your car every time you leave it, even for a few minutes. Amazingly, one car in five is left unlocked. If you live in a high risk area, ask your dealer about fitting deadlocks – this ensures that, even if a window is broken, a car cannot be opened by reaching in and releasing the door lock button. If your car does not have a built-in steering lock, buy one of the DIY kind and use it whenever you leave the car.

A lockable fuel cap will prevent thieves syphoning off your petrol and will force joy-riders to abandon your car when it has run out of petrol.

Lockable wheel nuts will stop thieves stealing your wheels.

Always remove the ignition key, even when you are parked in your own garage.

Radios and cassette players

Security-coded equipment is now available which means it has to have the code-number punched in before it will operate. Put the sticker provided in the car window to warn thieves. Some players are designed to be easily removed when the car is parked – if it can be removed, do it. Remember to retract your aerial whenever you are parked on the street – vandals love to snap them off, or bend them.

Window etching

Etch all the windows, wing mirrors, lights and any radio or hi-fi system with the registration number, and use a sticker to tell thieves that it has been done. It will not deter joy-riders, but it will put off a car thief, who will have to have all the glass expensively replaced. Many local police forces and crime prevention panels arrange etching sessions from time to time, and local garages often provide this service for their customers. If you want to do it yourself, you can buy an etching kit at a DIY store.

Valuables

Never leave anything – luggage, valuables or even coats on display inside a car: and that includes handbags, briefcases etc. If you have to leave things behind, lock them in the boot, out of sight. If you have an estate car, buy a cover for the luggage area. Never leave valuable possessions in the car overnight, even when it is parked in your own garage. And remember too to lock the car and remove the ignition key, even when it is parked in your own garage: garages do get broken into (see page 47) and a car full of valuables, with an ignition key in the lock, is a temptation no thief could resist.

Parking

If you have to park in the street, try to make sure the car is directly outside your house or flat, so that you will hear or see anything suspicious, such as a stranger loitering near your car. Fit a car alarm, and make sure it is on whenever you leave the car.

SIX

Alarm Systems

When you are looking at the security of your house, you must regard the various devices fitted – locks, bars, bolts, grilles etc. – as the first line of defence. Nothing is burglar-proof in the long run: what you hope is that your various defences will either act as a deterrent, or delay the burglar long enough for you to ring the police or otherwise summon help.

If the house is empty and the burglars are undisturbed, sooner or later they will find a way in. This is where your second line of defence – the burglar alarm – comes in.

One very good reason for having a burglar alarm is that the very presence of the alarm box on the outside of the house will act as a deterrent. It is a signal to the outside world that you are security-conscious and that the house is very probably fitted with good locks and other devices. It will certainly discourage the opportunist burglar, who will probably go off to find easier pickings elsewhere.

Even if he ignores (or fails to see) the alarm box, the chances are the burglar will run off the minute the alarm sounds – no burglar likes so much publicity. Even if the alarm doesn't go off until he has got inside, he is unlikely to linger once it does, and with luck, will go before he has had the chance to take much, or do much damage. It takes a very cool burglar to stay and ransack a house while the alarm is ringing.

Some people are put off alarms because of the number of false alarms they can give. If you live in a neighbourhood where alarms are constantly going off, eventually people stop paying any attention – with disastrous results when the alert turns out to be genuine.

If you are worried about that happening to you, or if your house is fairly isolated, with no near neighbours, you can enquire about having a system which is linked to a central command point. With professionally installed alarms, it is possible to incorporate devices such as automatic dialling equipment which will make an automatic 999 call and relay a pre-recorded message to the police when the alarm is triggered. Alternatively, the system can be connected through a digital communicator to a central station, run by the alarm company.

When it comes to choosing an alarm system, cost is obviously an important factor. Depending on how well off you are, and how much you want to spend, your choice ranges from a DIY alarm kit bought at your local hardware store, up to the personalised system devised and installed for you by a professional security firm. It is also important to choose a system which is reasonably easy to understand and operate. If the system is too cumbersome or too complicated, you will tend not to use it, especially when you are going out in a hurry.

Alarm system layouts

An alarm system can provide various degrees of coverage, and the more you are prepared to pay, the greater the protection you should expect. A basic system (**13a**) may protect only the ground-floor entry points, with sensors on the outside

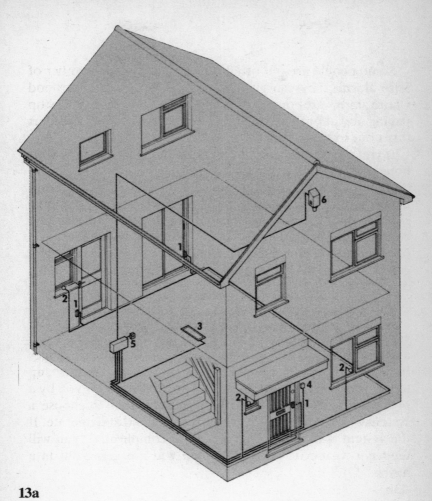

13a

doors (1) and windows (2), a panic alarm (4) by the main entry
door, and perhaps a judiciously placed pressure mat (3).
These are connected to the control box (5) which, in the event
of one of the sensors being activated, would operate the bell

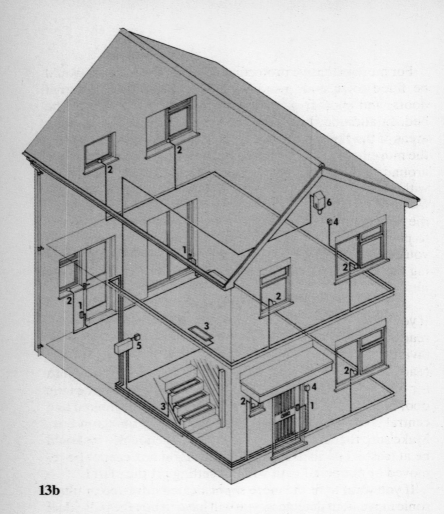

13b

or siren (6), mounted high and conspicuously on the wall. This layout may be perfectly adequate, especially if there is no access to upstairs windows, and can usually be extended at a later date.

For more extensive protection (**13b**), further sensors would be fitted to upstairs windows and maybe also to internal doors, and another panic alarm would be sited next to the bed. In addition, there may be "space" protection in some areas of the house provided by electronic devices that detect the movement of a person (see below). But how do you move around upstairs at night or open a window for ventilation without setting off the alarm? This is where a zoned system is essential – it allows you to switch off part of the system while the remainder is still activated. Obviously it is also important to plan a route from the bedroom to the control box so that you can switch off the system in the morning without producing the effect of a whole-house alarm clock!

DIY systems

If you want to install a DIY alarm system, you can either buy a ready-made kit, or you can assemble your own, buying the individual components and the cable. The advantage of the ready-made kit is that it comes complete with full instructions for fitting. The kit is likely to consist of traditional magnetic door and window sensors and pressure detectors, linked to a central control box which is linked in turn to an alarm box. Make sure that the alarm in the kit is loud enough – it should be at least 95 decibels – and that the alarm box cannot be removed or tampered with without setting off the alarm.

If you want to fit the more sophisticated infra-red or ultra-sonic movement detectors, you will have to buy the individual components and fit it together yourself. The system illustrated (**14**) shows how typical components are connected to the control box. Different circuits are run to different terminals, since some sensors break the continuity of the circuit

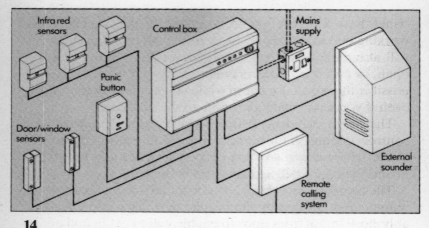

14

when they are triggered whereas others make (complete) the circuit. Wireless systems are available in which the sensors send a radio signal to the control box if they are triggered. Others are simply plugged into ring main power sockets to provide the circuit; any attempt to unplug them sets off the alarm.

The control panel

The control panel is the heart of the burglar alarm system: it enables you to set the alarm, switch it off and decide how much of the system is to be activated. It is important that you buy one where the operating procedure is simple and can be understood by everyone living in the house. If you go off for the weekend leaving teenagers, the au pair, Granny, Auntie Nell or whoever to look after the house, it is vitally important that they understand how the system works.

It is here that you set the alarm, either by using a key, or by typing a simple number code into a keypad. Most control panels have a facility for checking to see that all functions are working normally, and if not, alerting you to the problem. It will also alert you if any doors or windows have been left open, so that the detectors are in an 'open' position. It is not possible to give a false alarm while you are setting the alarm, even if you have made a mistake in the procedure.

There is an exit delay feature, which enables you to set the control unit and get out of the house without setting off the alarm. There is also an entry delay, which allows you to walk in and switch off before the alarm is sounded.

The control panel should be positioned where it cannot be immediately spotted by the burglar, but it has to be reasonably close to the front door to enable you to get in and out in the time allocated.

It is useful if you have a system with 'zone control' so that you can switch off a certain area of the system, such as the bedrooms, or the top floor of the house, to allow freedom of movement in one area while the alarm is protecting the other.

Usually, the control panel is powered through the mains, and is fitted with an automatic rechargeable battery which will power the system in the event of a power cut.

Magnetic door and window sensors

Magnetic reed sensors are the traditional detectors used for perimeter doors and windows. If the door or window is kept closed, the magnet keeps the switch inactive, while if the door or window is opened, the contact is released and a signal is sent to the control unit. Surface mounted switches are easy to fit, but can be tampered with. Recessed switches are best, being invisible when the door or window is closed, but it is not always possible to fit these, especially on some thin or metal windows or doors.

Inertia detectors

Basically, the device detects energy transmitted, created by force being exerted in the area where the device is fitted – ie a window being jemmied, a brick being chiselled out or an iron bar being sawn through etc. The inertia detector can usually give the earliest possible warning of an attempted forced entry.

Breaking-glass detectors

These are designed for large picture windows, patio doors etc. The device is quite small and unobtrusive and will offer protection up to approx. 3 feet (1 metre) radius from the sensor. The alarm is only triggered if the glass is broken or chipped.

Alarm noisemaker

This is designed for flat doors fitted with a mortise lock. It operates when considerable pressure has been applied to the outside of the door, activating the noisemaker before the door is forced open and scaring off the thief.

Movement detectors

Movement detectors are a very important part of the burglar alarm system. The traditional kind of movement detector is the pressure mat, a wafer-thin mat which sends a signal to the control unit when a certain amount of pressure is applied. The mat can only be used under a fitted carpet, and is usually placed inside the front and back doors, in front of windows, and on stair treads.

The more sophisticated movement detectors are wall-mounted and guard a wide area of a room. They need to be carefully installed and so are usually part of a professional installation.

Passive infra-red detectors

These work on the principle that all objects emit a certain amount of infra-red energy. The detector 'sees' the amount of radiation being emitted in a room. When the pattern changes, when a body passes through the area, for example, and the amount of radiation changes, the device sends an alarm signal to the control unit.

Ultrasonic movement detector

This is a device that uses ultrasonic sound as a method of detecting the movement of a body in a specific area. The device emits ultrasonic sound at a certain frequency, and a proportion of the sound is reflected back from various objects in the area. If a body moves in the protected area, the reflected pattern is disturbed and an alarm signal is generated and sent to the control unit.

Microwave movement detectors

The microwave detector uses the same principle as the ultrasonic movement detector and can be used to cover areas up to 100 feet (30 metres) in depth.

Panic alarms

These are also known as personal alarm switches. They are usually positioned beside the front door, and by the bedside, and are intended to be used to raise the alarm if an intruder is heard in the night, or if someone tries to force their way in. Panic buttons are permanently live and can be used at any time, even when your burglar alarm system is switched off.

Points about installation

Whether you are having the system installed professionally or doing it yourself, here are a few points to bear in mind when choosing the position of alarm components:

Panic alarms (15a) should be positioned where they can be operated without having to look for them. At the front door the alarm should be at the hinge side of the door so that, with the door chain or limiter hooked across, you cannot be restrained from using it. At the bedside it should be close to the bedhead so that you can reach it easily, without stretching, from the normal lying position.

An internal siren (15b) can be fitted in a position where it can

15a

15b

be heard in all parts of the house. Although the external bell or siren will be activated in the case of an alarm, double glazing and noise within the house can make it difficult to hear, especially from the far side of the house.

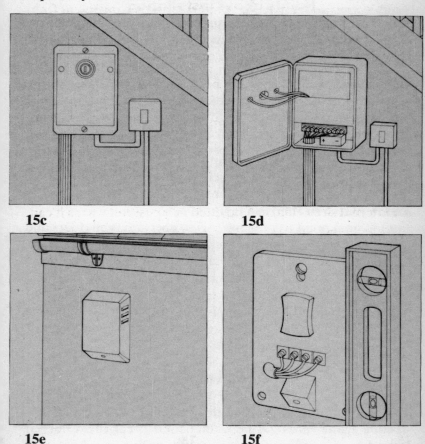

15c

15d

15e

15f

The control box (15c) should be sited where it can be reached within the time delay period after entering the front door, but where it would not be immediately evident to an intruder. A mains power supply will be required to operate the system (and charge up the back-up battery), and a convenient form of outlet is a fused connection unit – a plug can be removed inadvertently from a socket (to vacuum the stairs, for example) and not replaced. The mains cable must be kept separate from the circuit wiring of the alarm system (15d).

The external bell or siren must be mounted high up and prominently (15e), and out of reach from windows or drain pipes. If it contains an anti-tamper device, it is important that the unit is vertical (15f) to ensure that the device will operate correctly. Matching dummy bell boxes are often available as an extra visual deterrent on the other side of the house (without requiring further wiring).

One final point to remember is to check that all doors and windows, to which sensors are fitted, latch firmly in the fully closed position. It takes only a small amount of play in the catch to allow sufficient movement to activate the sensor. Remember too, before setting the alarm, to check that all latches are fully engaged to avoid false alarms. Those on internal doors are particularly prone to working their way open or being pushed by the cat.

Smoke alarms

Smoke alarms are an essential part of home security, not only as a safeguard against domestic accidents, but also as a protection against fires started when people break in. A burglar may drop cigarette ends, for example, or fires may be started deliberately by vandals. Fires often burn for more than five minutes before they are discovered. Smoke alarms will give you extra time to escape to safety.

There are two kinds of smoke alarms: ionisation detectors, and photoelectric cells. The ionisation type has a chamber enclosing two electrodes. When smoke enters the chamber, the flow of current is reduced and the alarm is activated. The photoelectric device contains a light beam and a photoelectric cell. When the beam encounters smoke, the alarm is triggered. There is a third kind which incorporates both techniques. Install alarms in rooms where fire is most likely to break out, with the exception of bathrooms and kitchens where steam or cooking fumes may trigger them off. A single alarm may be sufficient for a small house, but if your house has two or more storeys, it is sensible to place a detector in the hall, and on the ceiling of each landing. Make sure that the kind you choose conforms to British Standard 5446 Part 1.

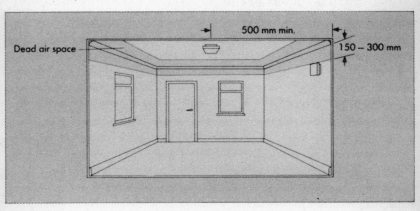

16a

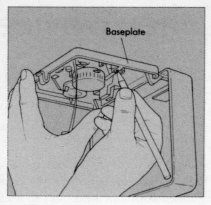

Baseplate

16b

When positioning the detector, it is important to avoid areas of dead air space (**16a**). Most of the air in a house is constantly moving through convection and ventilation, and it is this movement that carries the smoke to the detector. Round the edge of a ceiling above the level of windows and in the angle at the top of a sloping ceiling, however, the air is relatively still, and a detector placed here would not be activated before critical time had elapsed. Fitting is simplicity itself, by marking the screw positions through the baseplate (**16b**), drilling holes for the wall, or ceiling-fixings, and screwing in place. Make sure you test the alarm frequently to check when the battery is in need of replacement. Some smoke alarms can be interlinked so that they all sound when smoke is detected, and on more elaborate alarm systems there is also the facility to alert the fire brigade automatically.

SEVEN

Other Devices

The range of security devices on the market now can be quite bemusing for the average householder. As crime – and criminals – becomes more sophisticated, so the ideas from manufacturers proliferate. No one needs all the devices available, but if you shop around you will be able to devise a security 'package' that will suit you and your lifestyle – as well as your purse.

Remember that if you have any doubts you can always ask your local Crime Protection Officer for advice. He or she can give you the names of local security firms and may be able to arrange to visit your home to assess and advise you on how to make it more secure. As mentioned earlier, your first priority should be external doors and vulnerable windows – especially ground floor windows and any windows easily reached from the ground. Once these are secure, you can then turn your attention to some of these other devices.

Intercoms

The intercom is a simple way of enabling you to identify callers before you open the door. It is fitted beside the front door. Used in conjunction with a door viewer and a door chain you can then check any caller without running the risk of him or her barging in uninvited.

Entryphones

The entryphone is a more elaborate version of an intercom and fufils much the same function. This system is often installed in blocks of flats, and is ideal for people who live on their own, especially the elderly or disabled who may be afraid of callers forcing their way in after ringing the doorbell. The system consists of an intercom with a speaker/receiver and push button unit which is mounted at the front door, a remote door release on the front door and a telephone with door release button inside the house or flat.

Callers press the button on the entry panel beside the front door, which sounds a buzzer inside. When you pick up the phone inside, you can speak to the caller and find out who it is. If you decide to let the caller in, you press the button on the telephone which activates the remote door release. Unwelcome callers are left standing outside.

Entryphones can also be installed in detached houses fitted with a locked security gate. The phone is fitted on the gate, with an automatic opener as on a front door.

Remember, however, that entryphones and intercoms have not always been installed primarily or solely for security reasons: they usually also enable you to open a door or gate remotely, thereby perhaps sparing you the need to walk down corridors, or flights of stairs, or out into the garden. As physical deterrents to breaking and entering these systems are only as good as the strength of the doors, locks and mechanisms they control. And where they are used without offering an opportunity to make a visual check on your caller they can create risks caused by laziness or over-casual use.

In a large block, for example, it is entirely possible for an innocent and welcome caller to be followed in by one or more other visitors who are far from innocent – and whom the innocent caller may suppose to be genuine residents. A plausible story from a supposed tradesman or delivery boy can get the same effect. Never 'buzz open' the main door for a stranger without checking their story first. If you have not been able to make a visual check the importance of security procedure, and of being absolutely confident in the bona fides of a caller, becomes that much greater.

Similarly, never hold open the door for a stranger whose arrival coincides with your departure.

Audio-visual systems

A more sophisticated version of the entryphone combines a camera with a speech panel. Inside, the caller is shown on a tiny TV monitor, enabling you to identify him or her before pressing the door release button. This has the advantage of enabling you to tell if people are lying – the caller has no idea he or she is being observed, while you can see at a glance if it really is the postman, milkman, delivery boy etc.

Access control systems

These are most often used in office premises or in blocks of flats, but they are useful in any situation when you might otherwise have to supply lots of keys, with the need to change the locks if one falls into the wrong hands.

In the digital push-button type a panel is sited beside the front door. A pre-determined code has to be tapped out by the user before the electronic lock is activated and the door will open. The code can be altered very quickly to bar entry to anyone who does not know the new code.

Another version uses a 'credit card' type of key which is

inserted in a slot by the door, rather like using a bank card. The electronic code on the key is 'read' and the door is then opened if the code is correct. Card access units can be combined with push button units. Again, the access codes can be quickly changed to bar access to those who are no longer entitled to enter.

Standard features of this system include a device to prevent code-breaking by trial and error; adjustable entry times; and rechargeable cells in the event of a power cut. Some systems also include alarms to warn that unauthorised callers are trying to get in. Push button and card units are made for both indoor and outdoor use. They are usually weather and vandal proof and are easily programmable, with thousands of codes available to the user.

Safes

If you have small, very valuable items, such as precious ornaments, jewellery or documents, it is a good idea to keep them in a safe. Many people deposit their valuables with their bank, which will make a charge, depending on the size of the package or deed box you want to store, and how often you need access to it. As banking hours are rather limited, it is probably best to use the bank's facilities for documents etc. which you rarely need to see.

For jewellery and valuables which you might want to use or wear from time to time, it is better to use a safety deposit box, stored in an underground vault. These are available in most large towns and cities, and systems are run by the banks and by private security companies. Only you know what is in your safe deposit box. Usually, you pay for the box and for each visit to see it. Unlike banks, access is not restricted to banking hours, making it less inconvenient.

If you instal a safe at home, the first priority obviously is to tell as few people as possible about it, and then to try to ensure that a burglar will not find it.

Wall safes

These are designed to fit into cavity walls, replacing one, two or several bricks, according to size. They are made of steel plate and are drill-resistant over the whole lock area. Usually, they can be fitted with micro-switches for connection into alarm circuits. One ingenious version is a small cashbox-size safe disguised as a power socket; another looks just like a standard air-vent.

Before buying a safe, you will need to measure the thickness of the house wall. A convenient place to do this is in a window opening or doorway. Using three short lengths of batten, hold one flat against each surface of the wall and hold

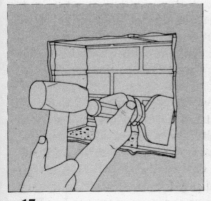
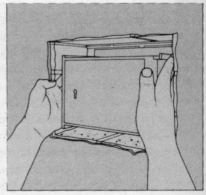

17a   **17b**

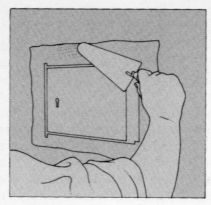

17c

the third one across them – through the opening. Mark the position of the inside faces of the first two battens – corresponding to the inner and outer surfaces of the wall – on the third batten. Measure the distance between the marks and deduct the thickness of any architrave around the opening to obtain the wall thickness. Fitting the safe involves cutting out the required number of bricks, using a brick bolster and club hammer (**17a**), wedging the safe in the opening (**17b**), and filling round the safe with a fine concrete mix (**17c**). When knocking holes in cavity walls, it is important to prevent any debris from falling into the cavity, otherwise it can cause damp to penetrate.

Don't make the mistake of hiding a safe behind a picture – the classic hiding place all burglars try. Choose an out-of-the-way position, in an unlikely room, and try to have it installed as firmly as possible. Remember that a burglar, if he finds it, might have no compunction about knocking it out bodily, removing it altogether, and working on it later when he has got away with it.

Floor safes

These are much easier to conceal and so are more secure. The best kind is made of steel and is set into a reinforced concrete floor. It is best to make a large hole, so that the safe is well embedded in concrete. Again, try to choose a room that is not obvious, the kitchen, say, but avoid rooms where the floor is likely to get wet, such as bathrooms.

Floor safes can also be fitted in wooden floors, but are obviously less secure than safes set in concrete. You have first to lift the floorboards: and the safe is designed to fit between adjacent joists and bolt or screw to them. You have to choose a position which is reasonably accessible without being an obvious hiding place. After the safe is fitted, the floorboards are replaced, cut and trimmed where necessary to fit round the safe. The safe is then covered with hardboard or plywood to bring the surface level with the surrounding floorboards. You can then cover the whole thing with carpet or a rug – but remember that burglars always look under rugs. A fitted carpet is probably more secure, if inconvenient.

Free-standing safes

If you have a lot of cash or valuables to protect, large free-standing safes are available. These have the obvious disadvantage of being hard to hide – all you can do is hope that they can withstand all attacks using explosives, drills, etc. Some safes claim to be resistant to oxy-arc, explosive and drilling methods and for extra security are fitted with spring-loaded relocking mechanisms which are set off if the safe is tampered with. Most safes can be anchored to the floor for added protection. A good domestic safe is fitted with a 7-lever keylock, but can also be fitted with a combination lock.

Property markers

Marked property is much less likely to be stolen, especially if you have a sticker in your window to that effect, and you have a much better chance of getting it back if it is stolen. Marking will also act as a deterrent, since it will be more difficult to dispose of the stolen goods.

The police recommend a property-marking code which is now recognised throughout the country. The code consists of your postcode, followed by the number of your house. If your house doesn't have a number, you add the first two letters of its name. So, if you live at 7 High Road, Newtown NT4 1AJ your code would be NT4 1AJ7. If you live at The Old Rectory, Newtown NT4 1AJ your code will be NT4 1AJTH. Use this code to mark all items of property that thieves go for – TVs, videos, hi-fi equipment, home computers, cameras, watches, jewellery, gold and silverware and antiques.

Security marking can be either visible and permanent etching and engraving, or invisible marking, which shows up under ultra-violet light. Engraving or etching can be done using a small tool, such as a carbide- or diamond-topped pencil (available from DIY stores) or you can buy a small electric-powered engraving tool. Most engravers come supplied with a stencil sheet of letters and numbers to enable you to get a neat result. Etching kits are ideal for marking glass, and punches are available for die-stamping a security mark on heavy metal items such as bicycle frames and tools. Indelible markers are used for fabric, while special pens are available for marking china and ceramics.

For antiques, which you don't want to damage, you can use an invisible marker which shows up only under ultra-violet light. The mark does fade, however, especially if the item is washed, so it will need to be renewed from time to time. You should also take colour photographs of valuable items which cannot be easily marked. Set each object against a contrasting background so that it shows up clearly, and lay a ruler beside it as a guide to size. This will be a great help to the police in identifying items if you are burgled.

Money and credit cards

Cash is *the* favourite target for thieves: it is instantly usable, requires no further negotiation, and is readily carried and concealed. Except in special circumstances, ownership of cash is difficult to dispute. So never keep large cash sums in the house, however well hidden, or in your handbag. Never leave your handbag or wallet just inside the front door, on the hall table, or on a window sill, where it could be seen from outside. Someone might be tempted to break the window and snatch it, or callers might spot it and try to get in on some pretext.

If your bag or wallet is stolen, ring the credit card companies immediately. There is a credit-card hotline to deal with this – keep the number handy (see page 124). Remember that thieves can use a credit card for telephone purchases, with little risk of being caught, and some shops only check credit cards over a certain amount. If you delay in reporting the loss you may be liable for a proportion of the cost of any goods fraudulently obtained. If you have a lot of credit cards, use one of the specialist companies which will cancel them all for you in the case of an emergency.

Always keep your cheque book and card separate – the thief needs both to write a cheque. And don't write down your PIN (personal identification number) with your cash cards where it can be found and recognised. Don't write it in your diary or address book – a thief will be bound to look there.

Lighting

Proper lighting can improve the security of your home in a number of ways. Adequate porch lights, front and back, will put off the burglar, who always prefers to work under cover of darkness. Time switches which control interior lights will protect the house while you are away, while photoelectric cells can provide lighting if an intruder enters the garden. Remember that after dark an unlit house looks very tempting to the burglar.

Time switches

If you are just going out for the evening, leaving some light on, in the bedroom and kitchen, say, is as good a deterrent as any (so long as you draw the curtains and leave a radio on, so that it doesn't become obvious that no one is in). The real problem arises when you are planning to go straight out for the evening after work, or if you are away for a weekend or even longer. You can hardly leave the curtains drawn and the lights on all day and night – it would soon become obvious what was going on.

The answer is an automatic timer. The simplest kind are plug-in socket timers. They plug into any socket and control a lamp or radio. You programme the timer to switch on and off at the times you want on a 24-hr dial. Another handy type is the electronic digital timer which can be set to four on/off settings per 24-hr day. If you are going away for a fortnight it might be better to vary the switching pattern. Anyone watching the house might realise how regular the pattern was. In this case you can use a 7-day timer where the timer can be set to come on and go off at different times each day.

If you want to switch on the main room lights, rather than just plug-in lamps, you can fit security wall switches, which replace the normal light switch. A programmable switch will switch the room light on and off at pre-set times. Photoelectric switches switch on the light at dusk and a timer can switch off the light at a pre-set time.

Outdoor lighting

Position outdoor lighting so that there are as few shadows as possible where an intruder could lurk. A light over the front and back doors is essential – burglars prefer to work in the dark – and the more enclosed and secluded your porch, the more important it is to keep it well lit. A side entrance with a gate should also be well lit. There is a wide range of outdoor light fittings available, including bulkhead and globe fittings for walls, ceiling lights for porches, wall-mounted lights for drives, garages and garden paths, and spike-mounted low level lights for general garden illumination.

Timers and photoelectric cells can be used to switch lights on at dusk, or at other pre-set times. An excellent security device is the passive infra-red sensor, fitted to the outside wall of the house. This sensor detects body heat and so senses the approach of an intruder, turning on the light automatically, an ideal deterrent for a patio or French windows – no burglar likes to be suddenly in the spotlight.

EIGHT

Neighbourhood Watch Schemes

Protecting your own home is fine, but you will enjoy greater security, and peace of mind, if everyone around you is working at it as well. The way to do it is to be a 'good neighbour', keeping a watchful eye on neighbours' homes as well as your own. By acting together with neighbours, friends and the police you can create a deterrent to the criminal. There is no doubt that crime prevention is most effective when it is a partnership between the police and the public. This is particularly true at the neighbourhood level, where a flow of information between public and the police is vital if criminal activity is to be foiled.

A tried and tested way of achieving this is by setting up a Neighbourhood Watch in your area. Without doubt, Neighbourhood Watch was *the* crime prevention story of the 80s. From the establishment of the first scheme in Cheshire in 1982 its growth has been phenomenal – currently there are 75,000 schemes, covering some 3.5 million households, and it is still growing: each year about 20,000 new schemes are set up. In rural areas a scheme might consist only of a few households, while in large urban areas there can be as many as 5,000 homes in a scheme. It is an impressive demonstration of the fact that ordinary people are not just concerned about the rising crime rate, but are prepared to do something about it.

The schemes have various names – Neighbourhood Watch, Home Watch, Community Watch – but they are all based on the same idea: improving the sense of safety, security and local community in an area.

How it works

Anyone can take the initiative in setting up their local Neighbourhood Watch, but before getting too involved, get in touch with your local police station. They will know what, if anything, is being done in the area. In many cases the police themselves set the ball rolling by canvassing with a leaflet and inviting those interested to a meeting.

If nothing is organised in your area, the police will help you set up an initial meeting to which local residents are invited – probably in your own home. Here the local Crime Prevention Officer will explain what Neighbourhood Watch is and find out how many people are interested in joining. If the response is suitably enthusiastic – and it usually is – an area co-ordinator will be found and people will be asked to volunteer as street co-ordinators.

Area co-ordinators

The area co-ordinator has no special skill or experience. He or she is simply an enthusiastic amateur whose task it is to liaise with the local police, organise a local newsletter and keep in touch with everyone in the scheme via the street co-ordinators. They will hold meetings of street co-ordinators from time to time to keep in touch with progress.

Examples of area co-ordinators are: a part-time nurse living in naval married quarters in Plymouth; a 63-year-old security officer in Sheffield; a teacher in Bedford who produces a newsletter with a circulation of 16,000; and a woman in Gateshead who has been an area co-ordinator since 1985. Working from her garden shed, she sends out a newsletter to 400 households on her council estate.

Street co-ordinators

It is up to the street co-ordinators to distribute newsletters, keep in close touch with their neighbours and report back to the area co-ordinators with news of problems, difficulties or successes. Everyone is encouraged to keep his or her eyes and ears open and report anything suspicious to the police.

There are three main elements to a scheme:

Vigilance Residents in a watch area are encouraged to be on the look-out for suspicious behaviour in and around the flats and houses in their area. The police are anxious to stress that Neighbourhood Watch is not intended to encourage people to 'have a go' or set themselves up as a group of vigilantes. It is intended to be a partnership between the public and the police. What the public provides are the local eyes and ears, but the police retain their active role when dealing with actual or suspected crime. The local Crime Prevention Officer will give advice on what to look out for, how to contact himself or the Home Beat Officer, and the kind of information the police need to have – detailed descriptions of a suspicious person or vehicle, car numbers etc.

Security At meetings, householders are given general advice by the local Crime Prevention Officer on how to improve the security of their homes. They can also invite the CPO to carry out a free security survey of their own homes, including advice on fitting locks, strengthening weak points, and, if necessary, recommending alarms. Members are also encouraged to look after the homes of other scheme members when they are away on business or on holiday.

Property marking The police strongly recommend property marking, and run demonstrations showing how the markers work and explaining the property marking code which is now nationally recognised (see page 74 for details of the code). The Metropolitan Police, for example, circulate a leaflet via Neighbourhood Watch called 'Mark It to Keep It'. It explains how property marking helps the police to trace stolen property and also acts as a deterrent: they provide stickers which you can put in your window advertising the fact that your property has been marked. As the leaflet says, once property is known to be marked, thieves think twice about stealing it.

It emphasises that for marking you should choose a surface that cannot be removed without spoiling the basic appearance or performance of the article – the burglar will then find it difficult to dispose of. The Metropolitan Police also supply a card, listing vulnerable items – videos, hi-fi, TVs, watches etc. – with columns where you can record details of make, serial numbers, value and where you have marked it. Such detailed information is a great help to the police if your possessions are stolen, and will help to identify and recover them.

Property markers are often owned by a Neighbourhood Watch Scheme, paid for by local fund-raising, or they might be donated by a local Crime Prevention Panel (see page 85).

Effect

The effect of setting up a Neighbourhood Watch scheme is usually instant. Most of the area co-ordinators interviewed talked of a drop in the crime rate of at least 50%. One says: 'In the year before we started, we had nine house break-ins in a 150-200 house area. In the first year of the watch, which covered 400 or so homes, this was reduced to one or two. Now we cover 700 properties, which is one of the largest in South Yorkshire, and we've only had two or three break-ins in the last 12 months.'

It brings home the point that the very existence of Neighbourhood Watch in your area will act as a deterrent, especially if it is well publicised with road signs and window stickers. But it is *not* the intention that members should deliberately attempt to scare off suspects. Observe discreetly, says the police advice, and report what you see. The fact that many calls from Neighbourhood Watch will turn out to be false alarms doesn't matter, say the police. The important thing is that the information supplied is accurate.

Once the scheme is under way it is important for organisers to keep up enthusiasm. Many schemes use newsletters to keep residents in touch with what is happening in their area. They can include the latest security advice, topical information about crimes in your area and any particular successes which your group has had. Also if there is a problem – such as a spate of connected burglaries or muggings – the police will alert the area co-ordinator who makes sure the information is passed on. To pay for the newsletter, the scheme might ask a local business to buy advertising space, or a member of the scheme might get permission from his firm to use a copier free of charge.

To co-ordinate Neighbourhood Watch schemes at a national level are the efforts of Crime Concern, the national crime prevention organization. A magazine "Good Neighbour" is produced quarterly and gives information about Neighbourhood Watch events nationally. It is produced by Security Publications and Crime Concern, and gives details of, for example, the 'Crack Crime' campaign and the recent 'Fear of Crime' conference. Over 250,000 copies of the magazine are distributed to schemes all over the country. If you would like to see a copy and keep in touch with activities, write to Good Neighbour, Security Publications Ltd, Argosy House, High Street, Orpington, Kent BR6 0LW.

A National Neighbourhood Watch Conference 1990, organized by Crime Concern, was held at Nottingham University's East Midland Conference Centre. Now that many schemes have been operating for several years, an important theme was how NW should develop in the 1990s.

The Conference programme will combine keynote presentations by national figures with talks by area co-ordinators from schemes which have carried out innovative and successful projects.

Social gatherings

NW area co-ordinators often organise street parties, picnics, coffee mornings etc. to enable people to get to know each other. It is a good way to make new friends – and will make it easier in future to spot strangers in the neighbourhood. Indeed, getting to know who your neighbours are, and the promotion of neighbourliness in general, are among the benefits and attractions of the scheme.

One good effect of NW is that it means there is much less

83

fear of crime. One area co-ordinator says: 'One very positive thing is that there's much less fear of crime, especially among the middle-aged and older folk. As a result, the co-operation of the local people is wonderful . . . Younger people are also involved – I have three or four teenagers who are street co-ordinators. They distribute the newsletters and check to see that the neighbours are all OK.' Another said, 'We take special care of the older people. Recently we've had a few younger folk pushing into old people's houses and robbing them. When the police told me I immediately rang all our people and we made sure that all the older folk were aware, and shouldn't open their doors unless they knew who it was. It stopped in three days – it was a very effective exercise.'

To sum up, NW helps people to feel less beleaguered: they are not alone with their locks and bolts and chains against the world. In a NW area anyone who is nervous or frightened knows that there are other people to call on, neighbours to watch out for him or her, and a Home Beat Officer and Crime Prevention Officer to give advice and reassurance.

Special constables

If you belong to Neighbourhood Watch, and would perhaps like to take a more active role in tackling crime, you could become a Special Constable. Recruited from ordinary citizens, Special Constables provide a police reserve. They are trained to undertake regular officers' routine duties when required and so free regular officers at times of emergency for special tasks.

As a Special Constable on duty you have the same re-sponsibilities and powers as a regular officer and wear a police uniform. Your local knowledge can be a valuable addition to police resources. For further information, ask at your local police station.

Crime prevention panels

Crime prevention will only be really effective when it has the full co-operation of everyone in the community. Crime Prevention Panels were designed to foster that co-operation by undertaking and supporting local crime prevention projects. Panels were first introduced in 1966, and there are now some 400 throughout the country.

Panels (usually of about 20 members) are usually made up of Neighbourhood Watch co-ordinators, members of tenants' and residents' associations, teachers, crime prevention officers, probation officers, directors of local companies, representatives of local newspapers, radio and TV etc.

The panel has to be aware of the particular crime problems in their area, relying on information supplied by the local police representative. The panel then has to decide how they can help to reduce these particular local problems, and a programme of work will be drawn up. Examples of projects have included:

■ Raising funds to buy security devices for the homes of the elderly and disadvantaged.

■ Joining forces with the local Chamber of Commerce and the police in an effort to reduce crime on local industrial estates.

■ Visits by panel members to the elderly following a spate of visits by tricksters posing as local officials.

■ Promoting property marking through the distribution of

leaflets and the sponsorship of marking pens.

■ Putting together a crime prevention roadshow, which tours local events.

■ Organising a poster competition in local schools with a crime prevention theme.

Like Neighbourhood Watch, the Crime Prevention Panels have devised a number of fund-raising schemes to support their projects, including obtaining sponsorship from local businesses. The annual Crime Prevention Panels conference is organized by Crime Concern.

Youth panels

There are also over 200 young people's crime prevention panels, either attached to an adult panel, or based on a local school. As well as educating young people about the effects of crime, the panels focus on crime prevention, particularly the crimes which affect them most directly, such as drug abuse and shoplifting.

If you are interested in joining a Crime Prevention Panel, or perhaps setting one up, contact the Crime Prevention Officer at your local police station, or write to Crime Concern (see page 125).

NINE

People Particularly at Risk

Everyone runs the risk of having their home burgled – the opportunist thief will strike wherever he can. But there are other hazards – unscrupulous thieves and villains who save themselves the trouble of breaking in by bluffing their way in, or even simply barging their way in. They may even have 'targeted' certain houses or flats, where the occupiers are known to be particularly vulnerable: the elderly, the disabled, women living on their own, and 'latchkey' children.

But if you are one of those people who are 'at risk', you don't have to live in a permanent state of fear of burglary or attack. There is a lot you can do to make both yourself and your home safe, and a lot of sensible precautions you can take against confidence tricksters.

The elderly

Crimes against the elderly, particularly violent crimes, get a lot of publicity, so that everyone gets the impression that such crimes are on the increase. In fact, this is not the case, but it is still true that the elderly are much more fearful of attack or burglary, and are much less able to cope if the worst happens and they are physically attacked or have their home wrecked and their savings stolen.

But the chances of becoming a victim can be much reduced.

If you have elderly relatives, or neighbours who are old and frail, you can help them to make their home safer. You could offer to fit additional door and window locks, door viewers and chains.

If you're elderly yourself, go round your house, as we suggested at the beginning of this book, and see how easy it would be for anyone to get in.

Ask yourself:

■ Is the front door strong enough? You can fit reinforcing strips which will strengthen the door frame, and you can also fit hinge bolts to prevent the door being forced open on the hinge side.

■ Are there bolts on your back door? Don't fit surface bolts which are easily slid back once the thief has broken through. Fit concealed security mortise bolts instead (see page 22).

■ Does your front door have a good lock? A simple spring latch is no good – it is easily forced, and the burglar can break a panel and reach in to undo it. You need a strong mortise lock or a surface-mounted rim lock which can be double-locked.

■ Do you have a door with glass panels, or a glass patio door at the back? Glass can easily be smashed to get at keys left in a mortise lock, or to operate the knob of an ordinary latch. Think of replacing the glass with laminated glass which will not shatter, even if struck very heavy blows.

■ Have you got a lock on your patio door? It should have locks top and bottom – and remember to remove the key.

■ Is the back door lock the original 'builder's lock'? These simple 2-lever mortise locks are too easy to pick. Fit a 5-lever one instead: you probably won't need to alter the holes, so there will be very little joinery work needed.

■ Have you got a door chain – and do you always remember to use it? Fit a strong door chain to help keep out unwelcome callers, and get into the habit of using it at all times.

■ Fit locks to all your downstairs windows, including locks on the stays of casement windows, and on any upstairs windows which are easily reached via drainpipes or a flat roof – including fanlights and skylights.

Finance

In some areas, pensioners who are hard up can get help with the cost of fitting door and window locks, and door chains. The London Borough of Merton, for instance, publishes a special Crime Protection Handbook for the elderly, and will pay a security grant to enable pensioners to install door viewers, door chains, window locks and door reinforcing strips. And in East Ham, one of London's largest Neighbourhood Watch schemes is playing a leading role in getting grant aid to fit locks on the homes of elderly people. Ask the Crime Prevention Officer at your local police station if there are any similar schemes in your area, or contact your local branch of one of the charity organisations such as Help the Aged and Age Concern.

Confidence tricksters

Some con men and confidence tricksters specialise in preying on the elderly, bluffing their way into their homes and tricking them into parting with cash or valuables. An essential first line of defence against tricksters is a door chain – and preferably a door viewer as well. Next, you must adopt a suspicious attitude towards any unexpected callers whom you don't know. Don't be worried or embarrassed about seeming rude or inhospitable – if the caller is genuine, he or she will understand, and won't mind being kept waiting while you check their credentials.

How to check strange callers

Think before you open the door, and put on the door chain. Next, ask who it is and what they want. Whoever they say they are, and whatever uniform they are wearing – police, council official, health visitor, gas man, electricity board official etc. – ask to see their identity card. Remember that friendly, smiling young women and children can also turn out to be tricksters.

Keep the chain on while you look at their card. Read it carefully – don't let yourself be harassed. If the caller gets impatient – be suspicious. Ask them to wait while you check their card by ringing the local office – don't rely on the number given on the card – it could belong to an accomplice. Check the number in your own directory.

If you can't get through or if you have any doubts at all, ask them to call back later, and arrange for a friend or relative to be present when they return. If you are worried in the meantime, ring your local police station and explain your suspicions.

Be suspicious too of any builders, odd job men or window cleaners who turn up unexpectedly offering to fix your guttering, mend the roof or do any odd jobs. Don't let them in 'to see the size of the job'. If you do need work done, ask them to leave a business card and tell them you will need references. If they supply references, make sure you check them out before you let them into the house. It's always better to use window cleaners, builders etc. who have been recommended to you by someone you can trust.

You should also be wary of anyone who calls at the door asking if you have any old furniture or pictures you would like to sell. Unscrupulous dealers have been known to call on old people, especially those living in small country towns and villages, in the hope of finding grandfather clocks, antique furniture, paintings and so on. Unfortunately, the owner often has no idea that his or her old clock, rocking chair, brass bedstead etc. is worth anything, and gratefully agrees when the dealer offers a few pounds 'to take it off your hands'.

You should refuse to answer any questions about your possessions and tell callers that it is none of their business. If they continue to call back and pester you, tell them you will call the police. This is where it pays to have a door viewer. If you see someone like that who constantly makes a nuisance of himself, you can simply not answer. Eventually, they will get the message and give up trying.

If you are perhaps short of money and would like to sell a picture or item of furniture, ask a reputable firm to value it for you. Get several quotations and don't accept the first offer that is made. Consult your family – if it is a family heirloom that you are selling, they may prefer to help you financially and keep it in the family.

Security checklist

■ Always put the chain on before you open the door.

■ If it's a stranger ask who they are and what they want.

■ Keep the chain on while you look at their identity card. Read it carefully.

■ If they claim to be from the police, council, gas board or electricity board, ring the local office and check that Mr or Ms X works for them. Don't be fooled by a uniform.

■ If the caller gets impatient – be suspicious.

■ If you have even the slightest doubt, ask them to call back later. Arrange for someone else to be in the house with you when they return.

■ If they seem bogus, or if you are at all worried, ring the local police station and explain the position.

■ Never keep large sums of money in the house. Your money is much safer in the bank, post office or building society.

■ Always lock up, even if you are only popping down to the shops for a minute.

■ Don't leave any lavatory or bathroom windows open when you go out. Thieves can get in through the smallest window.

■ Don't leave the kitchen window open so that the cat can get in and out – have a cat flap fitted instead.

■ Make sure the inside latch of your door can't be opened

through the letterbox.

■ Never give a stranger any information about any old furniture, ornaments or pictures you have in the house. Refuse to answer any questions and threaten to call the police if they pester you.

Women living alone

Women living alone are obviously vulnerable to unwelcome callers and people who might try to barge in, as well as strangers following them home and obscene phone calls. However, there is a lot you can do to minimise the risk, especially by taking commonsense precautions.

Start by making a check on the security of your house or flat, as described on pages 9-16. Single people are more likely to be living in a flat, so remember to pay particular attention to the strength of the door. Flat doors are often much thinner than the main front door, and can be easily forced or broken open. If your front door seems flimsy, consider replacing it with a much heavier one, or strengthen it with steel security strips (see page 18). Hinge bolts (see page 24) will also help strengthen the door, and prevent its being forced or levered off its hinges on the hinge side. Glass panels are particularly vulnerable – the thief can easily break the glass and reach in to unlock the door. First, replace any glass panels with laminated glass, which cannot be smashed, and secondly, make sure that the lock on your front door is adequate. A door chain will give protection against the 'barge-in' type of caller and a door viewer will enable you to vet all callers without them seeing you.

Door locks are covered in detail on pages 17-30, but basically you need a mortise deadlock, or an automatic rim dead-lock which can be locked from both the inside and outside. The important point to bear in mind is that the burglar should not be able to unlock the door from the inside if he does succeed in smashing a door panel, or an adjacent window. He will always want to unlock an exit door, a) to secure his exit and b) to enable him to carry out bulky items such as the TV etc. Again, make sure that all ground-floor windows have secure locks, including locks for casement stays, and all windows accessible from drainpipes or flat roofs – including skylights and fanlights – should also have locks. See pages 31-44 for detailed information on window locks.

If you live in a block of flats without an entryphone system, approach the landlord or other flat owners or tenants about installing one. It is an excellent way of vetting callers without them seeing you, and without having to have contact face to face. If your block does have an entryphone system, never let in a stranger who has some plausible excuse – ask them to write or leave a card. And never hold the door open for a stranger whose arrival just happens to coincide with your departure – he may have been lying in wait for an opportunity like that. If you are selling your home, try not to show people around on your own. Ask the estate agent to send a representative with any prospective buyer.

If someone does break in

What do you do if someone does break in to your house or flat? Waking up in the middle of the night to hear footsteps is a terrifying experience, especially if you are alone. If you do hear someone, don't just lie there and pretend to be asleep, but don't leap up to confront the intruder either – that could be very risky. Instead, switch on the lights and make a lot of noise. Call out to an imaginary relative or boyfriend. Most burglars will flee empty-handed rather than risk a confrontation.

If you ever come home to find a burglar in your house, never attempt to tackle him and never try to bar his escape route. Most burglars are interested in money, not gratuitous violence, but if cornered, a tense, edgy burglar may well turn violent to make his escape.

Remember too that you don't automatically have the right to use force on him, even though it is your home. If you injure him more than the situation seems to warrant, you would have to prove that you were acting in self-defence.

It's much better, however difficult it seems, to keep calm and humour him. Shouting and screaming are much more likely to make him violent. Concentrate on memorising as many details of his appearance as you can: this will be an enormous help to the police.

Coping with violence

If the worst happens and you *are* assaulted or raped, call the police as soon as you get the chance. Don't shower, wash or change your clothes, however much you may want to, because you will destroy vital evidence. Don't take alcohol or tranquilisers – you will need to be able to give a clear account of what happened. In many areas there are Victim Support Schemes to give you help and support in such circumstances – the police will be able to put you in touch with them. Don't be afraid to go to the police. They need your help to track down the attacker as soon as possible and stop him claiming more victims.

Don't be afraid to seek help even if it is someone in your own family who has assaulted you. The courts and the police have the power to deal with violence of this kind, even if criminal charges are not brought against him. But if you are the victim of domestic violence and you want the protection of a court order, you will have to be prepared to give evidence in court.

If you are afraid, or are worried about further assaults, you can seek help from your local Social Services Department. Ask for the address of any Women's Refuge in your area. Refuges don't publicise their addresses, to provide greater safety, but you will be able to get it from the Social Services Department – normally it has a 24-hour emergency phone number, which you can find in the local directory.

Security checklist

■ Always draw your curtains after dark to discourate peeping toms. If you think there is a prowler outside, don't go out to check – ring 999.

■ Only put your surname and initials in the telephone directory and on the doorplate if you live in a flat. That way, a stranger can't tell if a man or woman lives there.

■ If you think someone is following you home on foot, run to the nearest pub, laundrette or house with plenty of lights on. Don't call for help from a public phonebox – the attacker could trap you inside.

■ If you are being followed, never go straight to your front door. Go instead to a neighbour, pub, shop or police station. You don't want him to find out where you live, and you may not be quick enough about getting in.

■ If someone in a car is trailing you home, run away in the opposite direction to the one the car is facing.

■ Self-defence classes can help you to deal with an attack and will give much greater confidence. Ask your local police station or council if they run classes.

■ Neighbourhood Watch (see pages 78-86) is a great re-assurance to people living on their own. Find out from your local police station whether there is one in your area. If not, suggest that they start one up.

■ Cover up expensive looking jewellery when you are out: it could be an invitation to an attack, or the would-be thief may follow you home and note your address.

■ If you receive abusive or obscene phone calls put the phone down immediately and don't say anything. An emotional reaction is what the caller wants. Tell the police and the operator, and try to keep a record of the date and times of the calls to help trace the caller. If the nuisance persists, you may have to change your number and go ex-directory.

■ If you get home and find signs of a break-in – a broken window, say, or the door ajar, do not go in or call out: the intruder could still be inside. Go to a neighbour's house or flat and phone 999 from there.

Children and teenagers

Children should be taught NEVER to talk to strangers, and in the home, they should be taught NEVER to open the door to a stranger. If you have to go out to the shops and leave your children by themselves, make sure they understand that they must not open the door to anyone. If your children get back from school before you get back from work, and have to let themselves into the house, it is doubly important that they understand and obey this rule.

To help them, it's a very good idea to fit a door viewer and a door chain. That way, they can check who is at the door without having to open it at all. Tell them also not to answer the phone when you are out, in case they give away the fact that they are alone in the house. They should also know how to make a call to the emergency services, if necessary.

Be very careful when choosing a babysitter – child molesters have been known to advertise as babysitters. The best plan is to find a family friend who will sit in for you, or you could set up a 'babysitting circle' with some friends. If you must use a stranger, be sure to check their references. If you feel worried, ring home and ask to speak to your child. Be wary of men who always volunteer to babysit and who are obviously interested in the child's friendship. Always give the babysitter the number of a neighbour in case of problems, as well as the number where you or one of your family can be reached in an emergency.

Teenagers who babysit should always have arrangements made for getting home afterwards. If your child takes on a babysitting job through an advertisement, check it out for yourself, and ring during the course of the evening to check that all is well. Tell them to be very careful when working on a paper round: they should never accept if someone invites them in for a cup of tea or offers to give them a lift. Tell them to refuse politely and move on quickly.

If your teenager is going out to a concert or some such occasion for the evening, check what the transport arrangements are. If necessary, take them and bring them back yourself – it's worth the inconvenience for the peace of mind. Otherwise, give them the money for a taxi, rather than allowing them to wait alone at a bus stop. Tell them to take cabs only from a hire point, or after phoning a reputable firm. Make sure he/she has the numbers of a few local firms in case of need. Emphasise that they must never get into a car whose owner claims to be a taxidriver unless it comes from a hire firm or has a TAXI sign.

Always insist on knowing where your teenager is going, and get the phone number if possible. You may be unpopular, and will undoubtedly be accused of being a fusspot, but if the child fails to come home, you don't want to have to admit you had no idea even where he/she was supposed to be. Explain to your teenager exactly why you are worried. Get them to ring when they are leaving the concert/disco/party and tell you what's happening. Always encourage them to stay with a friend who lives nearby, rather than attempt a long journey home alone, late at night.

Security checklist

- Insist on always having a phone number or address when your teenagers go out.

- Check what transport arrangements, if any, have been made when teenagers go out. Give them the money for a taxi home if necessary.

- Be very careful when employing babysitters. Ask friends to recommend someone.

- Always provide the babysitter with emergency phone

numbers and the name of a friendly neighbour.

- ■ Impress on your children that they must never open the door to strangers.

- ■ Impress on your children they should never accept lifts from strangers or from someone they have just met.

- ■ Make sure your children know how to make an emergency phone call.

Insurance

With mortgage rates going ever higher, many householders are inevitably on a very tight budget and naturally look for every opportunity to keep down running costs. It is perhaps tempting to look at insurance as one of those optional items where the minimum possible should be spent, on the premise that 'it will never happen to me'.

Unfortunately, as this book has tried to make clear, 'it' is only too likely to happen, unless you take all the precautions; and one of the sensible precautions includes being properly insured. Otherwise, when the worst happens, you will have the added trauma of dipping into your savings (if any) to replace stolen items or repair structural damage.

Home buildings insurance

A home buildings insurance policy normally covers the structure of your home, plus permanent fixtures and fittings such as sanitary and bathroom fittings, kitchen units, fitted wardrobes and cupboards and interior decorations. Glass, in doors, windows and skylights, is also covered against breakage. Policies usually extend to include out-buildings such as garages, greenhouses and garden sheds. Limited cover is also given for boundary walls, fences, gates, paths, drives and swimming pools.

Most policies cover damage by fire, lightning, explosion, earthquake, theft, riot and malicious persons, storm and flood, aircraft or things falling from them, subsidence, landslip and heave, falling trees, impact by vehicle or animal, breakage or collapse of radio and TV aerials, escape of water from tanks and pipes and oil escaping from fixed heating installations.

A lot of people do not realise that their policy often gives some assistance towards alternative accommodation if they cannot continue to live at home as the result of an insured event. Generally up to 10% of the sum insured is paid towards the additional cost of alternative accommodation for you and your family. This cover proved a lifeline to families made homeless as the result of damage in the "Great Storm" of October 1987.

Excess payments

Some policies include what are called 'excess' payments – that is, an amount of money which you have to contribute towards the cost of each claim. Excesses vary in amount. They may apply only to certain types of damage, for example, storm or flood damage or the escape of water from tanks or pipes. One excess that appears in almost all policies applies to damage caused by subsidence, landslip or heave. This is usually a specific amount, eg £500, but may be a proportion of the rebuilding cost of your home.

Is your building insurance adequate?

The sum insured is the amount of money for which your home is covered, and is the most your insurer will pay under any circumstances, even if your home is totally destroyed. It is important that your sum insured is adequate, as most policies specify that the amount to be paid, even for less serious damage, can be reduced if there is under-insurance. Mortgage companies usually insist that you take out insurance, but that only covers their interest in the property. If you take out a mortgage of £30,000, it is not enough to be insured for that amount if the house actually cost £100,000.

Be warned – the market value of your house is not a reliable indicator of what the sum insured should be either. You should base your sum insured on the full rebuilding cost of your home to ensure that you are covered for the right amount. The rebuilding cost should include an allowance for permanent fittings, such as central heating, double glazing and additional charges such as professional fees. You must also add on an amount to take care of garages, fences, gates, paths and swimming pools.

How to make an estimate

Drawing up an accurate rebuilding cost is a matter for an expert – a surveyor or architect. However, the Building Cost Information Service of the Royal Institution of Chartered Surveyors has drawn up a chart which will give you a general indication of rebuilding costs. It gives rebuilding costs per square foot for five different house types: terraced house, semi-detached house, semi-detached bungalow, detached bungalow and detached house. It then gives costings depending on the age of the property, its size, and the area (London, South-East, East Anglia, East Midlands, Northern, North-West, South-West, West Midlands, Yorkshire and Humberside, Northern Ireland, Scotland and Wales). It also tells you how to work out the external floor area of your home, upstairs and downstairs.

The chart does not cover all properties – it excludes properties built of stone or other material than brick; properties of three or more storeys, or with basements and cellars, flats, and houses with special design features. Naturally, the rebuilding cost of even similar houses can vary depending on individual circumstances, but the table does nevertheless give a reasonable estimate.

If you would like a copy of this chart, to work out the rebuilding cost of your home, write to the Association of British Insurers, Aldermary House, Queen Street, London EC4N 1TT, enclosing a stamped addressed envelope, and ask for the leaflet *Buildings Insurance for Home Owners*.

Home contents insurance

Whether you own your home or rent it, you need insurance protection for its contents. Otherwise, if you are burgled, or your home is vandalised, or there is a fire, you will have to bear the total cost of replacing furniture, carpets, clothing etc. If you add up the value of just a few basic household items such as a cooker, fridge, washing machine, television and carpets, you will soon see that the total can be considerable. If you have been a home owner for 20 years or so, you are going to have virtually a lifetime's worth of possessions which you could not possibly replace out of your own pocket.

Normally, an insurance policy covers your furniture, furnishings, household goods, kitchen equipment and other appliances, food and drink, television sets, videos, computers and audio equipment, clothing, personal effects and valuables such as jewellery and personal money up to stated limits. In fact, just about everything you would take with you if you moved, apart from boats, caravans and cars, which are usually insured separately.

Most policies cover loss or damage to house contents by fire, theft, escape of water from tanks or pipes, oil leaking from central heating systems, storm, flood, subsidence, falling trees or aerials, riot or malicious damage, explosion, earthquake, and impact by aircraft, vehicles or animals.

There are two forms of cover available: *replacement-as-new* and *indemnity*.

Replacement-as-new

If you insure on a replacement-as-new basis, you will be paid the full cost of repairing damaged articles, or the cost of replacing them with equivalent new articles if they are stolen or destroyed.

Indemnity

For items covered on an indemnity basis, you will be paid the cost of repairing damaged articles or of replacing what has been stolen or destroyed, less an amount for wear and tear and depreciation.

Furniture, carpets, domestic appliances, television sets, videos and audio equipment can normally be insured on a replacement-as-new basis, but not usually clothing and household linen. As the property you can insure on this basis varies between insurers, and sometimes age limits apply, you should check your policy carefully.

Exceptions

There are exceptions to every policy. Read yours carefully and ask for an explanation if there is anything you do not understand. Common exclusions are theft if you have lent or let your house or part of it, unless there is a forced entry; sonic bangs; contamination by radioactivity from nuclear fuel or nuclear waste; riot and malicious acts occurring outside Scotland, England and Wales.

Is your contents insurance adequate?

The sum insured is the amount of money for which your home contents are covered and is the most they will pay, even if they are totally destroyed, say by fire. Your policy requires you to insure your contents for their value.

Some policies provide that, if you are under-insured, claim payments will be reduced. So remember, if your sum insured is too low, you may have to dip into your savings to put things right. To avoid this, you must get the sum insured right – this is *your* responsibility. The chart (pages 108-9) will help you work out the full value of the contents of your home:

Insurance discounts

Some insurance companies offer discounts for household contents premiums for policy holders who take certain security precautions. Normally, you can expect a certain percentage to be deducted from the basic cost of the premium, depending on the type of locks and other devices fitted. The percentage may also depend on the type of property, and its location – some areas are considered far higher risk than others.

If the company requires you to fit 'approved' locks, make sure you understand what they mean. And find out whether the insurance company requires locks and other security devices to be fitted professionally.

Companies that offer discounts:

Avon
Bishopsgate
Commercial Union
Cornhill
Eagle Star
Economic
Guardian Royal Exchange
Legal & General
National Employers Mutual
National Insurance & Guarantee
Northern Star
Norwich Union
Prudential
Royal
Sovereign Marine & General
Sun Alliance

Valuables: gold & silver articles, jewellery, furs, pictures, clocks, watches, cameras, ornaments, collections									
Sports equipment, books, cycles, records, computers, tapes, toys, musical instruments									
Garden furniture, lawn-mower, ladders, tools, paint, fuel									
Household linen: table linen, towels, bedding									
Clothing									
Other items									

If your policy is not index-linked, add on a suitable allowance for inflation.
You may, of course, have other rooms and possessions not listed here.   **TOTAL £**

Allowance for inflation during year at .... %

Your contents should be insured for   £

CHECK LIST	Lounge	Dining room	Kitchen	Hall, stairs	Landing and loft	Main bed-room	2nd bed-room	3rd bed-room	Bath-room/ Toilet	Garage & out-buildings	TOTALS
Carpets, rugs and floor coverings											
Furniture: tables, chairs, stools, settees, cabinets, sideboards, bookcases. Bedroom, bathroom and kitchen furniture											
Soft furnishings, curtains and their fittings, cushions											
Televisions, videos and audio equipment											
Household appliances: cooker, fridge/freezer, washing machine, vacuum cleaner, electrical goods, heaters											
Cooking utensils, cutlery, china, glass, food, drink											

ELEVEN

Squatters, Trespassers and Undesirable Tenants

Squatters, trespassers, undesirable lodgers, tenants who won't leave – all very different categories perhaps, but the net result is the same: people who are living in your house, or entering your property, against your wishes. Sometimes it can prove extremely difficult to get rid of these unwelcome visitors. How does the situation arise, and what can you do to prevent it?

Shutting up your house

What do you do if your firm decides to send you to Brussels, Saudi Arabia, or even the other end of the British Isles, for two or three years? You have the choice of leaving your house or flat empty and unused, or of letting it, using the rent to pay the mortgage and rates. Before the law was changed in 1965, no one dared to let their house during a long absence, in case they lost the right to possession. Now, the owner can let the house, use the money to pay the mortgage and outgoings, and be sure of getting it back, provided all the necessary precautions have been taken.

But many people can't be bothered with the fuss involved in letting: finding a suitable tenant, drawing up a contract, making a valuation of the furniture and fittings etc., putting things into store and so on. If you are only going to be away

110

for a relatively short time, three to six months, say, it seems much easier and simpler to put your valuables in the bank, cover the furniture with dust sheets, arrange for the gas, electricity and water to be disconnected, lock up securely, perhaps putting up shutters at the windows, cancel the milk and papers and go off without a care in the world.

Unfortunately, in these days of homeless families, a flat or house standing empty seems like an affront while thousands of people are roaming the streets, sleeping in hostels or bed and breakfast accommodation if they are lucky. A house standing empty and unoccupied is very obvious, but even in the case of a flat, someone will sooner or later notice that it seems deserted – junk mail will overflow out of the letter-box, circulars will pile up on the mat, the Post Office may leave new directories on the doorstep, and sooner or later the squatters will move in.

Squatters

Squatting is now a highly refined art, and in some London boroughs there are even leaflets available (in the public library) telling you what your rights are as a squatter. *The Squatter's Handbook*, published by the Advisory Service for Squatters, goes into the mechanics of squatting in great detail: how to spot a suitable property; how to get in without being prosecuted for 'criminal damage'; how to change the locks; how to deal with the police, if they arrive (ask to see their warrant); how to get gas, electricity and water reconnected; and what to do when the owner finally obtains a possession order against you. There are no helpful leaflets telling you how to get rid of squatters.

If you do arrive back to find squatters in residence who refuse to leave, try to remember (however enraged you might be) that it is a criminal offence to threaten or use violence to get into a house, even your own house (they will probably have changed the locks). However, if the squatters are out, you are entitled to enter, by force if necessary, and repossess your property. It might then be worth trying a bit of self-help, enlisting the help of a few well-built muscular friends to persuade them to go – providing you can get in. It's worth consulting the police, too, to see if the squatters are breaking the law in any other way.

Otherwise, what you have to do is institute court proceedings and have a possession order granted. The squatters will then be evicted by the bailiffs. Your local Citizens Advice Bureau will advise you on the procedure.

If the squatters have caused real damage, the court will probably order the squatters to pay compensation, as well as legal costs, though your chances of getting the money are probably slim. If the squatters are vagrants, or homeless, jobless people with no assets and no income, actually making them pay up may prove impossible in the end.

The legal process is notoriously slow. If you want to repossess your house quickly, you will have to see your solicitor and ask him about the 'quick procedure' route you can take, under Order 113 in the high court, or Order 24 in the county court, whereby you can gain repossession in a couple of days. If you think it likely that the squatters are going to resist, phone the police when you know the bailiffs are on the way and tell them what is happening and that there is likely to be a breach of the peace. The police will turn up to protect the bailiffs and this will make sure that the squatters do go.

Again, the court will almost certainly award costs and

damages in your favour, but getting the money will be very difficult.

All in all, having your house taken over by squatters is traumatic, time-consuming and expensive. Unless your house and its contents are fully insured (see below) you are likely to be severely out of pocket and – depending on how long the squatters were in residence – the damage could be quite extensive.

To be fair, squatters are more likely to choose empty council flats, boarded up and awaiting conversion, than a private house; but the longer your house is standing empty, the more it is likely to be at risk.

Prevention

Obviously, then, unless there are very good reasons indeed, you should *never* leave a house or flat standing empty and unoccupied for any length of time. Even if it is not squatted in, vandals will try to smash their way in, vagrants may light fires inside (not necessarily in the fireplace) youngsters will lark about and leave filthy debris – and you will return to find your home unoccupiable, open to the wind and the rain and in need of major repairs.

If you do have to leave your home empty for a few months, and you can't or won't let, one essential step is to tell the local police and to appoint someone – a friend, relative or trusted neighbour – to keep an eye on the property for you. It is important that any damage is repaired instantly – once someone has broken a window or forced a door, others will follow, attracted like a magnet by the thought of warmth and shelter, if not easy pickings. Youngsters, encouraged by the signs of neglect, may break in 'just for a laugh', light a fire, ransack the place looking for cigarettes or alcohol, and leave beer cans, graffiti and worse.

Insurance

There is another hazard attached to leaving your house for some time. Building and house contents insurance policies often have a restriction clause severely limiting the cover if you go away for longer than a stated period – usually 60 days. They will not then cover damage caused by thieves, vandalism, or accidents – so if your house was broken into, you would have no cover.

If you do have to leave your house for some time, you should let the insurance company know, whether you are planning to leave it empty, or let it. In either case, you must try to have your cover extended, though you will probably have to take out an extra policy to cover these special circumstances.

Letting your home

Suppose you decide to avoid the aforementioned horrors, and let your house? It will spare you worrying about squatters, but you must still be very careful. Even if you are only going away for a few months, be sure to draw up a contract or licence to let your home. Don't be sidetracked by the fact that you know the prospective tenant. He or she may even be an old friend but if things go wrong, if there is a disagreement, or a change in circumstances, the results could be very serious for you, the owner, if there is no proper contract. Always take legal advice before entering into any agreement, and always insist on having the agreement or contract drawn up professionally.

The various Rent Acts have given tenants a good many rights, as regards security of tenure, but special provisions were introduced in 1965 to enable an owner-occupier to let his or her home for a limited period, and have an absolute right to get the house back when he or she needs it.

To take advantage of these provisions, and to ensure you regain possession, you must give written notice to the tenant that you are the owner-occupier and that you are entitled to regain possession. The safest procedure is always to include this notice in the tenancy agreement or contract, and never to let the tenant have possession until the agreement has been signed.

Inventories

The contract you draw up must include an inventory of all the possessions, furniture etc. you have left in the house, and their value. Don't pack up your valuables or any treasured books, records, ornaments etc. and store them in the loft, or in a spare room. Your tenant may seem reliable, but you can't predict what his friends (or his successor) may do: curiosity might get the better of them eventually and if you are gone for longer than planned, the temptation to use (or raise cash on) your treasures may be irresistible.

It is wise to store valuables in a safe-deposit box or the bank, and to put particularly valuable pieces of furniture or ornaments into store, or ask a friend to store them for you. But be careful. Don't lose touch with friends or acquaintances who are storing things for you. All sorts of unforeseen things might happen: people might marry, divorce, separate, and in the process sell or divide up possessions. You may well find that your stay abroad turns out to be longer than planned.

After five years or so, is anyone going to remember that the grand piano belongs to you?

Suppose your friend died suddenly – would you be able to prove that the possessions or furniture stored in his house were yours? The executors of your friend's estate might quite reasonably maintain that the possessions are part of the estate, unless you could prove otherwise. It is always a good idea to seek legal advice before leaving valuable items with a friend, however well you know them.

To be on the safe side, draw up a list, with valuations, of all your possessions and where they are stored (bank, safe deposit, friends, furniture store etc.) and send a copy of this list to your friends, your solicitor and to your insurance company.

Another solution, if you can afford it, is to appoint Managing Agents who will manage the property for you in your absence. It then becomes their responsibility to ensure that tenants behave properly and pay their rent on time, to ensure that no damage is done to your house or contents, and that there is no problem over repossession when you return.

Changing tenants

If the tenant gives up the house before you return and he (or a friend) finds another tenant, there is no problem as long as the new tenant has written notice that you are the owner-occupier. Don't just sigh with relief if your tenant writes to say that he is leaving, but has found someone else to take over the tenancy. Again, it would be wise to arrange for a proper legal agreement to be drawn up, and also to arrange for someone to visit the property and assure themselves that all is in order. Make sure everyone understands that the written notice stating that you are the owner-occupier must not be overlooked when a new letting is being arranged on your behalf.

Repossession

When you return from abroad, or wherever, you will give the tenant notice to quit, and this has to be in accordance with the terms of the letting. It's a good idea to let the house monthly, or three monthly, rather than for a fixed number of years, so that if you come home early, you can give 1 month or 3 months' notice. Your tenant must then give up the house, and if he doesn't you can obtain an order for possession from the court – provided the correct procedure has been followed. In fact, the court can exercise its discretion if you failed to give the proper notices before letting your house, it is obviously better not to run the risk.

Retirement houses

There are other circumstances when you might want to let your house. If you are working abroad, you may well want to buy a house in this country for your retirement. Or you may live near your work, but plan to retire to the country/seaside or whatever. One day you see your dream home, and decide to buy it for your retirement. Can you safely let your house and be sure of getting it back when you are ready to retire?

The answer, fortunately, is yes. As before, you as owner can give the tenant notice of your right as owner-occupier to regain possession when you retire. This notice must be given before the tenancy begins or it can be included in the tenancy agreement (much safer). Never allow the tenant to take possession before the agreement is signed and exchanged, and as before, it is a good idea to obtain legal advice and to have the tenancy agreement drawn up by a solicitor.

Letting rooms or flats in your house

If your house is too big, now that the family is grown up, you may well decide to let out a part of the house as a separate flat, or to let off one or two rooms to lodgers. Some people may even buy a big house with the intention of letting off part of it to produce an income.

In all these cases the special provisions in the Rent Acts regarding owner-occupiers will apply, provided that you as owner are resident in the building.

This exception to the general rules giving security to tenants is because the behaviour of a tenant is obviously important when the owner is actually resident in the house. A bad tenant could make your life a misery. So, if your tenant is unreasonably dirty, noisy, badly behaved, or whatever, you are entitled to terminate the tenancy with a notice to quit. If the tenant doesn't leave after being given notice, you can obtain an order for possession from the court (consult your local Citizens Advice Bureau for details about the procedure). Proceedings are taken in the county court and though possession cannot be refused, the court has the power to postpone it for three months.

Since he is technically now a trespasser, you could try evicting him yourself, enlisting the help of a few tough friends, but what do you do with his property? If the tenant wants to be nasty, he can sue you for the loss of all sorts of imaginary and highly expensive items and you will have no way of proving that they were not in the house at the time.

Rent tribunal

The tenant has the right to refer the question of how much rent he should pay to the Rent Tribunal. This Tribunal, which controls all lettings, will decide what is a fair rent, and register it. Once a rent has been registered, that is the maximum rent you can charge, even if you get a new tenant. You can only increase the rent then by making a new application to the Rent Tribunal.

The tenant only has protection under the Rent Acts if he has 'exclusive possession' of his flat or apartment. But if the tenant shares 'essential living rooms' with you – say the kitchen, or a TV room – then he is no longer protected. Be careful though – a bathroom or toilet doesn't count as 'essential living rooms'. So even if your tenant shares these with you, he will still be protected by the Rent Acts.

Lodgers

There is a big difference between a tenant and a lodger so far as the law is concerned. With a tenant, it is much more important to observe the formalities, as discussed above, and to make sure that an agreement is properly drawn up. However, even with a lodger it is probably wise to make it clear, in writing, that you have the right to repossess the room whenever you choose. You should give the lodger a rent book, and ask for at least a week's money as a deposit.

A tenant can keep the owner of the property out of his rooms, or flat, but as the owner you have the right of access to the room of a lodger and cannot be prevented from entering it at any reasonable time. You can also exercise more control over the lodger as regards playing loud music, restricting the number of visitors etc.

Lodgers can often cause a lot of friction in a household when they fail to behave in the way you had expected. It is a good idea to spell out at the beginning what the rules are regarding use of telephone, bath, shower, washing machine, kitchen facilities etc., otherwise you can find yourself out of pocket.

If your lodger proves unbearable (or even if you are just fed up with him) you have the right as owner of the property to get rid of him. He has no rights to the room, and if he refuses to go, after reasonable notice, you can take legal action though it might be cheaper to just change the locks. However, be careful over the problem of his property. If he has a lot of expensive hi-fi equipment or whatever, get an independent witness to testify to what he has in his room in case there is a dispute later.

Trespassers

We tend to think of a trespasser as someone who enters our property without permission – someone who uses the garden as a shortcut, say – but a lodger who refuses to go when given notice, a tenant who won't move out after being given the correct notice, are also trespassers of a sort, along with squatters, burglars and so on. This is a very grey area. In theory you have the right to eject any trespasser, but a trespasser who did at one time have permission to be there (like the ex-tenant) is obviously different from a burglar or squatter who has never been allowed in.

The reality is that if you are an able-bodied male with lots of strong friends you will probably have no trouble in repossessing your own property. If you are a little old lady, your best idea is to go to the local county court. They will help you with the procedure, and they give priority to residential cases of this type.

If you are dealing with the problem on your own, you must first ask the trespasser to leave, and give him sufficient time to leave peacefully. If he refuses, then the owner, or someone acting on your behalf, and eject him. The trespasser can thus be ejected, but you are not allowed to use more than 'reasonable force'. A peaceful trespasser may be pushed, or grasped by the arm and urged to the door, but you are not allowed to punch or beat him otherwise you can be sued for assault. If the trespasser resists, and threatens to punch you, you are then entitled to defend yourself, though here again you are not allowed to use more force than is 'reasonable'.

When dealing with burglars the same rules apply. You can arrest a burglar and keep him held fast till the police arrive, but you can't shoot him or injure him. If the burglar resists, or fights back, you are allowed to use reasonable force to detain him, but if you injure him seriously, or even kill him, you then face a criminal prosecution, unless it was a clear case of self-defence. In practice the law tends to be lenient with people who use force on a burglar, provided they don't go too far.

TWELVE

Further Information

Security firms

Banham Alarms
11/15 Lillie Road
Fulham, London SW6 1TX
071-385 3322

Banham Patent Locks Ltd
233/5 Kensington High Street
London W8 6SF
071-937 4311

The Chubb Lock Company
PO Box 197, Wednesfield Road
Wolverhampton WV10 0ET

Ingersoll Locks Ltd
Forsyth Road
Woking
0902 637 788

National Supervisory Council for Intruder Alarms
St Ives House, St Ives Road
Maidenhead, Berks SL6 1RD
Maidenhead 37512

Insurance

Association of British Insurers
Aldermary House, 10-15 Queen Street
London EC4N 1TT
071-248 4477

Women

Rape Crisis Centres will offer help and counselling. If no number is given in your local telephone directory, you can find the nearest centre by phoning 071-837 1600 (day and night) or 031 556 9437 (Scotland)

Victim Support Schemes: ask the police to put you in touch with the nearest group

Citizens Advice Bureaux: they can help you find legal advice, and where necessary, legal aid. Look in the telephone directory for your local office

Women's Refuge: The Social Services Department can put you in touch with your nearest refuge, if you need somewhere to shelter from violence

The elderly

Help the Aged
St James's Walk
London EC1R OBE
071-250 3399 (advice line) or
031-556 4666 (Scotland)

Age Concern
Bernard Sunley House
60 Pitcairn House
Mitcham, Surrey CR4 3LL
081-640 5431 or
031 228 5656 (Scotland)

Children
Childline (free national helpline) 0800 1111
Freepost 1111
London EC4B 4BB

KIDSCAPE
82 Brook Street
London W1Y 1YG
071-493 9845

Incest Crisis Line 081-422 5100 or 081-890 4732

Mothers of Abused Children 0965 31432

Credit cards
(numbers to ring if they are stolen)
Barclaycard 0604 230230
Access 0702 352255
Diners Club 0252 513500
American Express 0273 696933 (office hours) or 081-551 1111
(outside office hours)

General Information

Home Office
Crime Prevention Unit
50 Queen Anne's Gate
London SW1H 9AT

Crime Concern
David Murray John Building
Brunel Centre
Swindon
Wilts SN1 1LY

OTHER TITLES IN THE SERIES:

Coping with Children's Ailments
Dr Kilya Kovar

Choosing a Name for Your Baby
Edited by Suzy Powling

Counting Your Calories
Dr Patricia Judd & Dr Gabi Reaidi

Getting the Best From Your Microwave
Joan Hood

How to Buy and Sell Your Home
Michael Stock,
National Association of Citizens' Advice Bureaux

How to Get a Job
Bill Lubbock and Richard Stokes

How to Pass Exams
C. M. Hills

How to Pass Your Driving Test
John Thorpe

Planning Your Wedding
Joyce Robbins

The Highway Code: Your Questions Answered
Wendy Goss

Understanding Body Language
Jane Lyle

Knowing Your Rights: A Guide to Consumer Law
Vincent Powell-Smith, David Clarke, John Parkinson,
Richard Townshend-Smith, Christine Willmore.

How to Invest Your Money
John Morgan

How to Get Published
Neil Wenborn

Increase Your Word Power
Stephen Curtis

Test Your IQ
Victor Serebriakoff

Setting Up Your Own Business
Alan Pitman

Coping with Stress
Helen Dore

Planning Your Retirement
David Hobman

The Consumer's Handbook
Jean McGlone

Secure Your Home

Writing Letters for all Occasions
Joyce Robbins

Looking After Your Cat
Wendy Goss